THE
Little Book of
BIG EXCUSES

THE
Little Book of
BIG EXCUSES

More Strategies and Techniques for Faking It

Addie Johnson

Conari Press

First published in 2007 by Conari Press,
an imprint of Red Wheel/Weiser, LLC
With offices at:
500 Third Street, Suite 230
San Francisco, CA 94107
www.redwheelweiser.com

Library of Congress Cataloging-in-Publication Data
Johnson, Addie.
  The little book of big excuses : more strategies
and techniques for faking it / Addie Johnson.
       p. cm.
  ISBN-13: 978-1-57324-313-1 (alk. paper)
  ISBN-10: 1-57324-313-2 (alk. paper)
  1. Excuses--Humor. I. Title.
  PN6231.E87J64 2007
  818'.602--dc22

                                    2006100807

Cover and text design by Anne Carter
Typeset in ITC Century
Illustrations by Anne Carter

Printed in Canada
TCP
10 9 8 7 6 5 4 3 2 1

Contents

Chapter 1

Stretching

THE

Truth

A man may not be responsible for his actions in
an hour of tribulations and pain.

TALMUD

Making excuses is as old a practice as any in society. From the first time time that anyone behaved badly and wished they hadn't, or didn't do what they were told, we humans have handily created more and better ways of covering our asses. Some are teeny nothings—you come up with them and then forget them in an instant. Some are more weighty and take some time and imagination to compose. Whatever the case, if you need an excuse, and believe me, we all need one (or ten), you've come to the right place.

Just don't feel like giving out your phone number? Or scrubbing the toilet? Or paying your taxes? Make your excuses, and get out of almost anything in style. Or at least put it off. Embrace your inner escape artist and weasel out of the confines of daily drudgery and into the bright sun of slacking off.

Maybe you need an advanced excuse, an excuse for, you might say, the inexcusable. Have to leave someone at the altar? Sent a nasty email about her to your mother-in-law by mistake? Haven't filed taxes since 1987? It's happened to the best of us. This little book will give you some starter ideas, some examples from excuse-meisters, and quite a few excuses you should probably not use under any circumstances at all.

Warning: This book is not going to make you a better person. In fact, it could very well make you a worse person. Angry all the time? Annoyed with your boss, your kids, your parents? Too much stuff to do? I don't think this book can solve all your problems. Or maybe it can. But it sounds like it's time to laugh it off and slack it off and renew and rejuvenate. Maybe a nice bubble bath? Maybe a nap? I think it's time to stop letting that to-do list get the better of you. Time to fight back with some ingenuity and maybe some silliness.

C'mon, admit it. You know a horrendously bad person lurks inside each and every one of us—that person who doesn't want to clean the garage, have tea with her great aunts, eat his vegetables, or serve on a jury.

So this book is an invitation to fool some of the people some of the time. Face it—sooner or later, a messy situation is going to arise, and you're going to want to squirm out of it. It could be a missed deadline at work. It could be a blind date with your Uncle Tom by marriage's great nephew who farts, or at least he did the one other time you met him when he was six and you were seven.

In the case of the former, you may want to fake a sick day. In the case of the latter, you may want to plead a really heavy load at work. And then when you next run into said nephew at a family dinner and realize what you've missed, why you just may need to call in sick so you can spend his last day in town with him.

Now I think I hear a little voice inside you. Ooh, yeah, here it comes now. It's your conscience. It may be telling you, *Don't listen to her! She's a dastardly miscreant liar and she's leading you down her path of deceit.* To which I say, *phooey.* Your conscience has an overdeveloped sense of the dramatic. But kudos for having one. I like to think of it as creative fibbing. You're not lying— you're stretching the truth. You have a moral muscle, and I think it could use some limbering up with a healthy dose of humor. And stretching is good for you. Like yoga. And stuff.

I also think this conscience thing might be mouthing off because you have an underdeveloped sense of entitlement. Um, hello? As you make your way on the journey of life, there will be crappy times and fabulous times, and they both might get in the way of your doing all the stuff you're supposed to do. So get out there and get out of it, already. You deserve it. Besides, everyone else is doing it.

Basic Guidelines

We all make excuses. This book is just here to help you make them and make them better. You may be thinking, "Gee, Addie, I've been trying to cut down on making excuses and take more responsibility for my life and my actions." And to you I say, "Go on with your righteous self. This book may not be for you." But if you're saying, "Hey, Addie, I'd really like to cut down on getting *caught* making excuses," I say to you, "Bravo! Go ahead—make more excuses and more believable ones for things you don't want to do so that you can really focus in on the things that are truly worthy of your time and energy."

Let's break it down—there are so many wonderful and effective ways to excuse yourself. Embrace the following guidelines for everything from the most trivial to the most blatant excuse, and you will never be left out in the cold.

First, there's **actual innocence**. I'm presuming you will not be using this excuse, because you are a big faker and you are reading this book because you need some big fake excuses. But, as they say, "It's not a lie if you really believe it." This is the mantra of the pathological liar and you may adopt it as needed. Believe your lies, at least a little bit, at least while you are telling them, and then have enough respect to remember them later.

I didn't do it! You can always claim it wasn't you who ate the cheese or pushed your little sister off the sofa or even say that nobody did it at all. My cousin's husband claims that if he breaks a dish and she doesn't notice for 48 hours or more, it's as if the dish never existed. Also, you can always claim you've been framed. Like when the copier jams at work, or they run out of sugar packets at the donut shop. These are clearly frame-ups.

I didn't mean to do it! (a.k.a. I didn't know what I was doing.) Maybe your mental capacity was diminished—your short-term memory has been on the fritz so how could you be expected to know you wouldn't have enough funds in your account to cover that check? Also maybe you're too young and inexperienced to know better. Or, too old and experienced to know better.

Whoops! It's not my fault. Okay, you did it and you really can't get out of admitting the fact. But it's totally not your fault. If you don't partake in the monthly martini gathering at your in-laws, they will make your life a living hell. And once you're there you're so nervous that you have to get bombed, and if you bonk yourself on the bedpost as you fall into bed fully clothed, this seems to me to be a just fine excuse for having a black eye. And therefore staying home from work. For at least one day.

> Occasionally, honesty is the best policy. But use it sparingly, and only when absolutely appropriate.

I had to do it! Yes, you did it and you will own up to the fact, but you were perfectly justified. You didn't clean your room because your baby brother needs a floor padded with all your clothes so that he can learn to walk and fall down without hurting himself. Besides, you said I didn't have to clean it until we had company!

The Honest Excuse

Occasionally, honesty is the best policy. I can't believe I just said that. But use it sparingly, and only when absolutely appropriate. Seriously, sometimes the truth makes a great excuse. Like when Guy Ritchie told a bunch of students at Oxford why his movie *Swept Away* starring his wife Madonna was going straight to video in England. "People think it's s——."

You'll also want to try and build a chain of credible excuses, preferably one that cross-references other excuses you've used in the past. E.g., you have a phobia of mice (excuse 1) so you haven't been able to face taking care of the infestation in your ceiling at home, so you're going to need the day off work to wait for the exterminator (excuse 2) while sitting outside in your car in the driveway with your dog who is just as frightened as you are of the infernal things. And then because of all the upheaval, your dog will probably need some special park time over the weekend (excuse 3) so you can't babysit for your cousin's three maniacal rugrats after all.

In general, the first rule of excuses is that the devil is in the details. I mean, the *truth* is in the details. Or the "truth," as I like to call it. As you create a credible story, it must be filled with juicy tidbits to back it up. In fact, in some cases, the more outlandish and ridiculous the lie, the more readily it will be believed. I think this is the fundamental principle of writing advertising copy, by the way.

The second rule of excuses is *remember your lies.* I cannot stress this enough. Most of us are not pathological liars, so we tell a lie here and there, and then we trip up and spill the beans. Knock it off! You gotta remember what you've said. This will also help you avoid the embarrassing situation of using the same excuse too often.

For this reason, remember that exaggeration is your friend. From exaggeration is born the "sort of true" excuse. This excuse is easy to come up with, because it's true. It really

Remember your lies! I cannot stress this enough. Most of us are not pathological liars, so we tell a lie here and there, and then we trip up and spill the beans.

happened to you, or someone you know, or someone you read about, or watched on TV. Or some version of it happened to someone, somewhere once, so why not you? I know a woman who was pulled over for speeding along the highway. When the officer came to her window, she had worked herself into a half weeping state and explained that she was rushing to pick up her son Ollie from the hospital. She didn't mention that Ollie was actually her dog, and the "hospital" was her little code word for doggie day care. To her credit, Ollie *had* been pining away for her there all day, and she *was* late. But more importantly, she didn't get a ticket.

If you have trouble remembering your lies, you need to write them down in a little book. You also need to keep this book on your person at all times, lest it should fall into the wrong hands.

So, those are the basic rules. Be specific and remember what you said. Write it down if you have to. Write down the excuses you've used not to turn up for family dinners, office events, second dates—all the illnesses and their variations that have kept you away. You might also write down interesting things that could have happened to the email, the check, the gym membership card. Write down your childhood phobias—why you can't possibly clean the bathtub, for instance (okay there was a HUGE spider in there once).

Write them all down. You never know when they might come in handy. And read on. Pretty soon you'll be a regular Gold Medal Excusist. You'll be able to adapt the excuses in this book to the circumstances of your own life on the fly.

Some Pitfalls

It is better to offer no excuse than a bad one.

GEORGE WASHINGTON

Excuse Hazards to Avoid

Recurring Excuses: This is a tricky one. You should not, under any circumstances, use the same excuse two years running for forgetting, for example, to send your mom something or to call her or to spend time with her on Mother's Day. And that excuse should not be "It's a made-up holiday, invented by BIG Card Co. in order to make money." Because A) you are not going to uninvent it by being all snotty, and B) your mother deserves better, even if she too is of the opinion that it's mostly a made-up holiday, etc. So maybe one year your big bad boss made you work all day. And maybe the next year you came down with a little Sunday-all-day flu. *No, Mom, it was not caused by my social activities on Saturday night!*

After you read this book, you can probably do better than that second lame-o excuse. Maybe the dog ate the flowers. But under no circumstances, if you are so clueless as to forget Mother's Day two years running, should you use the same excuse.

11

However, do remember your "phobias" and "allergies." Say your best friend asks you to bring shrimp cocktail for her dinner party. And you forget. And you show up empty-handed.

Don't bring other people into it—unless they know what you're up to and have pledged to back you up in every way until the end of time.

Well, you were on the way to the fish market, in fact going in the door, when you remembered the last time you had shrimp. You were ten, say, and it was Christmas Eve and your dad wanted you to try it. And you ate a piece and your throat started to swell up and you got red and itchy and your parents got you to the emergency room just in time. And just as you were walking into the fish market you remembered that you were never supposed to touch shrimp, even wrapped up in paper and plastic. So what could you do? You didn't want to ruin her party by having to go to the emergency room. And you didn't want to get anything else, because you know how particular she is about her menu.

Don't bring other people into it—unless they know what you're up to and have pledged to back you up in every way until the end of time.

You should know this, but it's an incredibly common mistake. Don't discuss anything you might have to prove, like:

Emergency Room visits or hospital stays*

Jury duty

Doctor's visits

Funerals*

Divorce decrees

Don't go overboard with your symptoms or your details.

You want to have copious amounts of both, but they've got to be believable. Nobody calls in sick with the flu and has headache, nausea, ringing in the ears, vertigo, and tingly hands. And if you do have all that going on, it's time to go to Mr. Emergency Room.

Don't laugh.

Under no circumstances should a liar begin laughing at any point during the delivery of a lie. Really. Not even a little bit. Don't. Never ever.

Throughout this book, I will offer advice for transforming bad excuses into really great ones, so we'll do some little excuse clinics. Here's an easy one to get you started.

Excuse Clinic, kindergarten level:

Bad: Jack couldn't come to school today, signed "my mom."

Better: Jack missed school yesterday because he had bronco-it is. Signed, Tom Mix

Best: Please excuse Jack Frost from school yesterday. He has a cold and was running a fever. Signed "Mrs. Frost."

Excuse Clinic, upper level:

As we will see later, the lame-ass excuse certainly has its place, but don't go trying to use one stupid reason as an excuse for something even stupider. For example, even if it's true, this is BAD: "I'm late because I got drunk last night and married my cousin."

It's bad that you're late, it's worse that you got too drunk, and to top it all off, you're a redneck idiot who probably needs glasses and definitely needs a blood test. You want to go the opposite way with your excuses, from bad to better to best.

So, distance yourself, make it a little better, and cast yourself in a better role:

"I'm sorry I'm late. My cousin got drunk last night and married her high school boyfriend, and somehow I got roped into being the best man."

Or, to really do it up right: "I'm sorry I'm late. I was the designated driver and had to take my drunk cousin home from her own quickie wedding in Vegas last night. And when she woke up this morning and realized what she had done, I had to help her find a really good lawyer."

Don't come up with something people will hate you for.

You want to come up with something that will make people feel slightly sorry for you, but not implicate yourself in anything too awful, like chronic drug use or embezzlement. If you are caught, you'd better think fast and come up with the best Good Samaritan reason you can: I'm in jail and didn't make it to the wedding out of state because I was caught smuggling marijuana across state lines in my underwear and was charged with felony possession. But I had to try to bring the weed to my aunt who suffers from persistent, chronic, nonspecific nausea. (Never admit she's a hoot to get high with. You have never inhaled.)

And don't come up with something people will hate you for. We don't feel sorry for you that you have to go shopping with your mom when she's in town. We don't care how annoying she is. You're getting free stuff. Shut up.

So, onward. Don't waste your time feeling guilty about missing that social event, or office picnic, or whole work week. Excuse yourself in a way that will leave everyone impressed with what a wonderful person you are, or feeling slightly sorry for you, or both. Are bad excuses, or worse *no excuse at all*, hurting the feelings of those you love or are otherwise beholden to? Step up to the plate, people. Fib a little, limber up your moral muscle, and, best of all, get away with it!

Chapter 2

Fake, DON'T Flake

Excuses for Not Showing Up

You don't want to be known as a flake. Especially if you are of the blonde persuasion. And I don't care if it comes out of a bottle or takes three hours at the salon every six weeks. If you start to be unreliable about showing up to places, you're going to get a reputation. To flake is immature and childish. People are waiting on you, even depending on you. So if you can't face showing up, you're going to have to fake. Faking requires some thought, even ingenuity, but believe me, it's worth the effort.

For instance, your grandma won't understand if you don't show up at her birthday luncheon—unless you explain that you have been asked to escort Hillary Clinton when she comes to town for a fundraiser. Assuming she's a diehard Democrat, that is. But do not go overboard. Do not be tempted to say you will make it up to her by getting an autographed photo of the two of you for her mantelpiece. That just creates a big old problem and then you'll actually have to go track down Hil and maybe make a big contribution, and if it's going to get that complicated, you might as well just go and have lunch with a bunch of eighty-year-olds. Actually, you could probably learn a lot from those ladies.

And surely your boss will understand that you need to skip the team-building trip to the ropes course because it happens to conflict with your grandfather's birthday. (You don't need to say it would be his 110th if the dear man were still among us. May he rest in peace!)

And of course, there's faking being sick so you don't have to go to work. Everything from allergies to migraines to a flare-up of that irritable bowel syndrome. But not just calling in to work-there are so many occasions that call for a flake-out. When your friends and family want your help—moving, doing chores, babysitting. When you can't face the seventeenth holiday party this month. When you feel like your head will explode if you have to volunteer for one more event at church or the kids' daycare. There are not enough hours in the day to get the most basic working/sleeping/eating/bathing ratio down. You clearly already have enough to do, so get flakin'.

The Basics

A lot of this chapter is about flaking on work. Also known as calling in fake sick. You'll want to read up on this further in *The Sick Day Handbook*, also from Conari Press. Apparently, calling in fake sick is on the rise. Probably because people are getting fewer sick days and personal days, and traffic is so bad that after you've worked nine hours and spent another three hours commuting, you have twelve hours left in your day to eat, do laundry, sleep, and have a social life. If you're like me, you sacrifice sleep first, but after a month or so of not getting enough, it's time to call in sick just to lie in bed all day. Almost everyone has called in sick with a bogus excuse at one point or another, so why not you? I can hear your mother and mine in the background, "Would you jump off a bridge if everyone else was doing it? Well, Mom, it depends on the height of the bridge and the water conditions below, as well as air and water temperatures factored against the potential embarrassment of being the only one left standing on the bridge. So there."

Getting fake sick can help you get out of almost anything in style. Know your symptoms and KISS—keep it simple, sickie. If you've got a cold, rough up your voice a bit on the phone, or rub your eyes if you're faking the onset of an allergy attack that will get you out of going to dinner tonight with your husband's golf buddies. But don't get carried away.

Someone told me about their coworker who thought he was getting all fancy-pants and it backfired on him. He called his boss early in the morning with a bad case of diarrhea. He phoned from the

If you're calling in fake sick to work always opt for something semi-chronic: vertigo, asthma, arthritis, etc.

bathroom, where he had several glasses of water on hand, so he could make realistic sound effects as they talked. Everything went fine until he dropped a glass into the toilet by accident and it shattered. His boss gasped on the other end, "Oh my god. What was that?" But he was laughing so hard by this point it was all he could do to blurt out, "I'm sure I'll be feeling better tomorrow" and hang up quickly. Lucky for him, the boss said nothing the next day and he got away with it. Whew.

In terms of illnesses, I always opt for something that's semi-chronic, at least at work where people don't know you very well. By this I mean you want to talk about your allergies, your vertigo, your asthma, your arthritis any chance you get. These can all have symptoms that are not necessarily visible, and they also can have particularly bad and painful moments, also known as "flare-ups" or "episodes." Talk about your symptoms at slightly awkward moments. This will make people uncomfortable and less likely to want to get to know you, which will also have the added bonus of getting you off the hook for social occasions with coworkers.

Don't just confine yourself to illness—injury can be a good excuse too. Like the time I didn't get back to work the day after my vacation because I went jet skiing and stepped off the jet ski on a coral reef and got a sea urchin spikes stuck in my foot and had to go to the emergency room to get them removed.

Someone else I know had to take three days off for a cat bite. It was really serious. He let it go too long and it got infected and he had to have infusions of antibiotics every six hours. He almost lost his hand. Fortunately, he made a full recovery. Unfortunately, everyone at the office meowed at him for the next month.

If you're older, you might use this one not only for work but for any other task that requires the use of your fingers. I used to work with an older woman who would call in sick after gardening, and she would say that her pinky finger hurt so bad that she couldn't type. Rheumatoid arthritis is the real deal.

Beyond Getting Fake Sick

There are lots of other good reasons to get out of stuff. I'll just make a little listy, and you can pick and choose what suits you, and maybe some will inspire you to create your own that are even better.

- Your oldest friend came into town last minute and is only going to be here for one day.

- You got free tickets to the opera, baseball game, wrestling match, or dog show. How can you pass that up?

- Someone had to leave their baby with you due to an emergency—you can get a sound-effects CD at any music store and blare it in the background for added effect.

- Family members, real or imagined. Crazy uncle? Sick father-in-law? Be specific, and if you do make someone up, stick with it. Consider them an actual member of the family. Talk about them a lot, cut a picture out of a magazine so that you have a mental image of their face. This way you are less likely to slip up and forget they exist. (I once missed a wedding because my crazy great-uncle Jimmy threatened to "blow up the plane" because he thought the airline employees were being rude to him. Well, as you can imagine, we spent several hours being interrogated by FAA security and missed our flight and are now on a list of dangerous persons so we get questioned whenever we go anywhere. Thanks Uncle Jimmy.)

- Your landlord illegally shut off your electricity.

- You accidentally drove through the automatic garage door before it opened. This could happen, but if it does you're probably really tired and you should stay home and get some rest.

Sometimes a lame excuse works wonders, like:

I have a sick kid. The adult goats, however, seem to be doing fine.

This kind of excuse works best on people who have a developed and committed sense of humor. Note: those in positions of authority often do NOT have this advanced sense of humor. Bear with them. Their lives are more difficult and tedious because of it.

A child—drum roll please—is the jackpot as far as excuses go. And an infant? You've won the lottery. Megamillions of excuses there. For not showing up places, for not being bright and fresh as a daisy. Fathers get no sleep for at least six months to a year, mothers haven't slept since their first trimester so tack on an additional six months of sleep deprivation there. And we all know what sleep deprivation can do. It's so effective as a form of torture that people will literally say anything to get some sleep after a few days. Social faux pas? Your mental function is severely impaired and you don't have to take the blame. There is also some scientific evidence to suggest that quick to follow the infant and then the placenta in shedding itself during the birthing process is the brain itself. Or at least some of its major functioning. I swear, I read it somewhere.

And for the animal lover in all of us, animals provide endless good excuses for all kinds of things:

- "My horse has colic."

- "I promised my cat I'd spend the whole weekend with her." (And if your date still wants to go out with you after that, there's something very wrong with him.)

- "I need to clean the terrarium."

- "I caught a cold from my goldfish, and I wouldn't want to give it to you." (See promises to cats.)

- "I didn't bring a salad because my guinea pig started to cry when I opened the refrigerator."

- If you live near a beach you might be late because you had to wait for the mama sea turtle and her 250 babies to cross the road. (Ducks also work, but turtles are slower.)

Out-of-Control Excuses

Sometimes life throws a curve ball at you. Or sometimes it doesn't, but you can think back to all those times it has in the past, and summon up that feeling of precarious uncertainty. Then you can take a deep breath and go all Zen and embrace the moment as you realize there's nothing you can do, and you'll just have to let it go. So will anyone else who's depending on you. There's nothing they can do either.

- "I'm ovulating today, so I won't be in." (You can't help it. If you want to get preggers, you gotta do what you gotta do.)

- "I took Tylenol 3 with codeine instead of a vitamin, because the bottles looked alike."

- "My brother's snake got loose and I'm afraid to leave the bedroom until he gets home."

- "The Goddess didn't wake me." (Use only if you have established that you are the kind of person who expects that a higher power will wake you when you are ready. Or if you have a cat named The Goddess.)

- If you live in the country on a dirt road, you can claim they were grading the road and you got stuck behind the truck and had to turn around and go home.

- If there's a big storm in your area maybe a tree fell down and came through your window or onto your car.

- "The ghosts in my house kept me up all night."

- "I had to drive to Nebraska to pick up my daughter because her dad is in jail."

- "The doorknob fell off my front door, and I'm locked in."

Excuse Clinic

Have to go to a co-worker's birthday party? You hardly even know them, and they expect you to pay for dinner *and* bring a gift? Or it's your turn to host the book club gathering and you just can't face it? You can always use the excuse that your family is in town, and this is OK, but maybe we can make it better.

Better: "My brother just got kicked out by his girl-friend so he's staying with us for a while."

Best: "My brother's girlfriend is trying to kill him so he has a restraining order, but he brought his dogs to our house and he's going to be staying with us for a while because we have an alarm system."

A Really Bad Day

If it's one of those days (weeks, months) where the universe just seems to have it out for you, come up with a good excuse and stay home!

Sometimes, all you need is a series of semi-awful things to happen and it just puts you over the edge. The universe just has it out for you. Come up with a good excuse (if your ruinous life isn't providing you with enough already) and stay home, my goodness. The people who are depending on you will understand why you had no choice when you launch into these tales of woe. People understand this. We've all had those days, where you stepped in a big pile of bad luck, and no matter what you do you can't seem to wipe it off.

My most recent one went like this (totally true story): I woke up late because the alarm was set for 7:30 p.m. instead of a.m. As I was running through the house trying to get ready, I slipped in the bathroom and fell right on my tail bone. After covering up three pimples and trying to fluff my greasy hair, I left the house. Without my wallet. And when I turned around to go get it, I realized it was sitting right next to my keys and I was locked out. After that, a bunch of crazy stuff happened at work, including a visit to Human Resources to mediate a dispute between myself and a coworker that had escalated out of control about some sour milk she threw away in my paper recycling bin. After scrounging

"My housemate put food in my shoes."

in my desk for enough change to buy some soup for lunch, I was hit by a bike messenger while crossing the street and the soup spilled all over me, scalding my legs but missing him completely. At this point, I should have gone home, but I had an appointment after work to pick up my taxes from the accountant. When I got there I learned that I owed $4,372 to the IRS because of a mistake on my W2. That day sucked, and I can tell you I used it as an excuse for getting out of stuff for weeks afterward.

This last one I overheard in a restaurant. This guy showed up several hours late to work and offered this simple, yet tantalizing excuse: My housemate put food in my shoes.

There could be so many interesting stories behind this one, and yet, that's all the information he really needs to get off the hook.

The Really Totally LEGIT (more or less) Excuse

There are a couple of reasons to skip out on work or school that hardly count as excuses, they're so legit. You could actually earn some time off by busting your butt and coming in early or staying late for a week or two and actually getting some stuff done. And by "getting some stuff done" I don't mean beating your high score in Tetris. Once you've proved yourself, you could even ask for a day or two off. Your boss will probably be so blown away by your work ethic and your honesty, that she'll happily oblige. You could also ask to work from home for a day or two. Then you can do some work without ever getting out of your p.j.'s and you don't have to sit on the bus or subway or in traffic.

Now, if you are a student I hope you have taken advantage of the opportunity to skip school to go to a political protest or rally. Particularly if you are a social science, poli-sci, or government major, and even if you have taken any of these classes or plan to maybe take one of them someday in the future. They can't argue with that. You are skipping class so you can personally battle the tyrannous apathy that clutches the youth of our nation in a vise-like grip of inaction. You are proactively taking a stand, hand in hand with your brothers and sisters for a better world. How could an hour or two of class, a paper, or a test, begin to measure up to the service you are doing for yourself and your people? Besides, many of your superiors were children of the lost generation. If they scoff when you question authority and challenge the status quo, they're total hypocrites.

Excuses for Being Late

Obviously you can use a lot of the excuses we've covered so far for being late, too. But here are some more.

The Bridge Made Me Late

Not every city has a bridge, but if you are so lucky to live in one that does, bridges offer many excuses for being late. From the more obvious, to the "use only in season."

- "Bridge traffic was backed up for an hour, they said on the radio. So I just turned around and went home."

- "I got onto the bridge and traffic was so backed up we sat there for a long time. I'm really sorry—I left the house in plenty of time. I think someone was going to jump. It was awful. I remember the time my second cousin threatened suicide." (Sniff a little here. Do not be tempted to elaborate on your cousin. Just accept a little sympathy.)

- "I saw the sign 'Bridge freezes sooner than roadway.' I got on the bridge and, man, my car started to go out of control, and I had to go real, real, real slow. So that's why I'm late."

- "I watched the news and the river is going to crest tomorrow, so I won't be able to drive over the bridge to work." (Never mind that your route doesn't take you anywhere close to the river or the bridge. They don't need to know that.)

Weather

Wet stuff, dry winds, ice and snow, or a heat wave. All can be adapted to suit your lateness needs.

"Truth" Is Stranger than Fiction

My friend Polly told me, "I once told my film professor I was late because I had to put on my makeup. There was a long pause as he looked at me and took in the fact that I wasn't wearing any makeup and also had a black eye."

"My car broke down. The gas tank was leaking gas all over the road. And with the price of gas and what you pay me to work here, I had to lie under the damn thing with a collection device made out of an empty coke bottle and a Styrofoam coffee cup."

"My dog was hit by a go-cart."

There are times when you are lucky enough to be witness to something so wonderfully (or horrifically) absurd that you may want to use it as an excuse. In fact, you'd be remiss in not sharing the details, even if you have to go all the way home and get your camera for proof. (It's okay too if it makes you even later.) But you'd better have a good picture when you get there, or be prepared to explain that your camera was out of batteries or something. In our day and age of digital recording devices, every citizen is a man-on-the-street reporter covering the action as it happens. It's practically your civic duty as a member of our overblown live-news-feed society. You can also try and fabricate this kind of excuse, but as they say, truth is stranger than fiction, so make it pretty weird.

The Long-Term Flake-Out Fake-Out

Occasionally you might find yourself in the position of needing some real time off. A free trip around the world, an offer to work for three months in Italy, a little time to collect unemployment while you write that screenplay you've always dreamed about. If for some reason you can't share the details of the real reason you're going, and you want to leave your job and come back in a couple of months, or if you're a freelancer and you would like to work for these people again someday, read on:

Faking having to go to a far-away funeral is a bullet-proof excuse for sneaking off on vacation. Just don't come back with a tan.

You are going on a pilgrimage to Mecca, or Rome, or Mount Kailash. Choose your own adventure, but it's religious freedom—they can't hold it against you.

Maybe say you are doing some charity work. Earthquake, poverty, AIDS, tidal wave relief work. I personally couldn't use this one without spending at least part of my time off actually doing some of this work, but to each his own moral compass—know what I'm saying?

And this one is so devious I wish I could take the credit, but I heard it second hand:

Get to a large newspaper dealer that carries international newspapers. Buy the main one in your destination country and find someone in the obituary section to adopt as your beloved deceased aunt. Tell your boss (or whoever else you're trying to get away from) that the preparations and funeral and wake ceremonies will take at least a week and that your family is incredibly close (in that old world kind of way) and would never forgive you if you stayed home. Do your vacationing and, while you're there, get some of those little mass cards from that funeral. Just show up toward the end of the funeral—there are always spare cards hanging about. Show them off when you get back and talk in some (minor) detail about your aunt. You might also bring a cheesy gift for your boss, just as icing on the cake.

Chapter 3

Try

THIS

at Home

Household Excuses

Sometimes I play a little game with myself. It goes like this. I make a to-do list. One of those big, all-encompassing monsters with everything on it that goes on for at least two pages. Then I calculate how much time I think it might take to do each task, and I pencil that number of minutes in next to each entry. When I'm done, I add it all up and the number is inevitably so staggering (last time it was upwards of 96 hours) that I just have to take a nap to regain my composure.

We are all so busy. There is so much to do. In olden days when times were simpler, we were also busy and we worked hard but most things could eventually get done. If you had to plow a field or knit a sweater, you just got to it. Not so now. Everything has to get done with backup paperwork, a quick Swiffering of the bathroom, and at least two trips to get supplies/rations, sorted into the proper bins, getting permits, and picking up the kids from soccer, dance, and Tai Kwan Do. Plus 16 emails and 8 phone calls. And as we all know, it is one of the steadfast laws of the universe that the busier you are, the more messy your surroundings become. For example, I am on deadline for this book, and the dust bunnies under the bed are currently forming an alliance with the bits of food on the plates stacked in the sink in a nefarious plot to overtake the entire contents of the refrigerator. I'll show them—there's nothing in there but a bit of icky cheese and some really old horseradish.

You are not a pack rat, you are a collector.

Or maybe you are a pack rat. There are plenty of good excuses for this. If you keep every outfit you ever bought from the time you were, say, 16, you'll never ever have to say, "Wow, look at those jodhpurs back in style, and I used to have a pair just like them." You'll have them. (Warning: It may be a bit depressing to try them on. So just having them is enough. You might not need to actually wear them.)

You are not a pack rat, you are a collector—with lots of interests. The boxes of papers and art projects that date back through kindergarten are going to become part of your masterpiece—a collage of your life—someday. Meantime, they're packed in boxes in the back closet.

You are not addicted to buying things you don't need at garage sales. You are buying up things that will be collectibles and antiques by the time you're ready to open your own little store.

So here is a little to-do list, and some pretty darn good reasons not to accomplish a single thing on it. Taking a nap is not lazy. It is work that you need to do to make up for your sleep debt, which, like the national debt, is only growing every moment you are awake and is sure to make you pay big time down the road.

To do, or not to do. That is the question. Whether 'tis nobler in the mind to suffer the grime and clutter of outrageous upkeep, or to take brooms against a sea of dust mites and, by ascrubbing, end them. Well, when that Hamlet guy tried to fix his problems, everybody ended up dead. Don't go there, for goodness sake.

To Do

Laundry
Okay, I didn't do the laundry because after I got home from work and changed clothes and micro-ed some din-

ner and watched TV and talked on the phone, well it was getting late, and it takes a long time to do the laundry, and I don't want to disturb that nice lady in 2C, right next to the laundry room. I'm pretty sure she goes to bed at 9:00. So tomorrow night maybe, no, wait . . . there's no soap, I have no quarters, and frankly why bother if there's still one pair of semi-clean socks?

To do, or not to do, that is the question.

Mow the lawn

So, dad/honey? I read somewhere that this area hosted all kinds of native prairie grasses at one time. Then we came along and started trying to grow genetically modified grass and stuff that doesn't belong here. But, if you let your lawn go for seven years or so, well then it will be back to its natural habitat. (This is an excuse that could last for a good long time. But I wouldn't count on it.)

Practice piano

Instead of practicing, I'll dream about playing the piano. I read somewhere that's what the great musicians do.

Do homework

The school has no funding, so we have to share our books and we can't take them home with us at night.

41

Make dessert

My soufflé fell, my whipped cream soured, and my rhubarb pie sent three people to the hospital. I think we'll go out for ice cream.

Scrub the toilet

My friend Bash can't scrub the toilet because it makes her dry heave.

Finish unpacking from the last time we moved

We're just going to move again anyway someday. If I haven't looked for anything in those boxes in the six months we've lived here, I can probably just throw them out unopened, right?

Take out the garbage

It's too cold. Or it's too hot. In the town where I was born, the collectors got a bit big for their britches at one time and refused to pick up certain people's garbage on certain days. And they would leave a note with the reason: "Too stinky." Hello!? It's *garbage*.

Clean the garage/rain gutters/minivan

These tasks are full-day projects. As soon as you have a full day with no plans at all, you'll get right on it. (Then you'd better get busy filling up your social calendar.)

Clean up bedroom

My room isn't messy, this is a work of ART! Or a science experiment, if there's any old food in there.

Deal with the termite infestation

What termites? There are no termites in this part of the country.

Scoop the litter box

I wasn't wearing my glasses, so when I peeked in the box it looked clean to me.

Change the toilet paper roll

This is an age-old art passed only via secret ceremony from mothers to daughters when they venture out on their own. No male knows the secret, and you wouldn't want to disturb the delicate balance.

For moms: I'm always the one to change the toilet paper roll. I'm just going to let it sit on the sink. Then someone will feel really bad when it falls in and they have to fish it out and bring it to the garbage. I have to teach them a lesson somehow.

Clean out the refrigerator

I'm allergic to mold. And half-eaten sandwiches. Note: the common household is rife with allergy triggers—pet hair, mold, dust, dirty socks—so you can use this one on more than just the fridge.

Wash dishes

I can't do dishes because when I was a child my grandmother was washing wine glasses and broke one and it nearly severed two of the tendons in her left hand. I have undergone years of therapy and am currently immersing my hands in soapy water for 15 minutes per day, but if I hear the sound of a dish breaking I hit the ground and yell at the top of my lungs. It's not pretty. Better to avoid the dishes completely.

It's Not My Fault

And here are some for the kids, to use on your parents. Or parents can use them on kids. Or spouses and housemates can use them on each other. These are the "it's not my mess, my fault, my responsibility" excuses. And have you felt the presence of the dirty dishes ghost?

So many home tasks require preparation. And often, though the task may be fully and undeniably your responsibility, the preparation is not. Like, you can't do the laundry if your husband, who is responsible for the shopping, keeps forgetting to get laundry soap. (You might give yourself a boost by forgetting to add laundry soap to the shopping list.)

Or, if you read the good book: see Leviticus 18:10. "The nakedness of thy son's daughter, or of thy daughter's daughter, even their nakedness thou shalt not uncover: for theirs is thine own nakedness." Oops—can't change my grandchild's diapers—by biblical injunction. So sorry.

Not me.

I had a childhood friend we'll call Sam, because that was his name and I don't think he'd mind me telling this story. Sam's family had a cat. The cat had a perfectly good name, something like Sparky, I don't remember exactly what (it's not the pertinent part of the story, okay?). Anyway, one day a carton of milk was dropped in the kitchen. "Sam," his mom asked, "who spilled the milk?"

Sam, being quick on his feet, answered, "Sparky." This went on. Who forgot to flush the toilet? Pick up the toys. Who broke the glass? Let the tub overflow? You got it: Sparky. Sparky did so many things that Sam's mom renamed the cat. His new name: Scapegoat.

Any time anybody in that family spilled, dropped, or forgot something, they had a built-in excuse,

"Scapegoat did it." I'm fairly certain, though, that Scapegoat didn't climb by himself into the laundry chute and end up in the basement a bit worse for wear. But I couldn't swear to it.

Nagging

Maybe the to-do list above is not of your own devising. Maybe your partner, or parent, or roommate came up with the list and expects you to make a significant contribution to its execution. Yikes, this could get ugly. After you've used every excuse you can think up, you may experience some nagging. This is perfectly normal. I encourage you, however, not to be swayed from your course. Just let it wash over you. Give in to the demands of a nagger and you'll never be free. Stay strong and ignore. Smile politely and nod, and then adjust your earplugs when they turn away.

Party Cleaning

Okay, so maybe you've reached a moment of truth. When certain things can't be put off any longer. You get a call that your in-laws are driving over for a quick visit, or your husband is bringing home a client for dinner, or maybe time just got away from you and it's time for your annual winter cocktail soiree. You have to go from not doing anything at all to doing as little as possible to make your home look presentable—and fast.

Everybody, let's have a party cleaning! This is the kind of cleaning you do when your house is a filthy pigsty and you have to get it ready in 15 minutes for "company" as my grandmother would say. You've had a busy week, your kids have been sick, the dog ate a whole box of crayons and has been having multicolored diarrhea all over the house. Whatever the actual excuse, it just won't do. The house had just better look presentable.

How to Do It

Picking Up

First do a sweep of the place picking up stuff that can be thrown away, including old newspapers, plastic bags, water bottles. Other optional throwaway items include: bills (if you trash it, is it still due?), socks with any kind of hole (darning is no longer a feasible practice), ugly presents from relatives who do not understand you or your sense of décor). As you do this, you can also make piles of things that need to be moved, like any socks you aren't throwing away will have to go in the laundry hamper, but just put them in a pile on the first pass and then go back through the house picking up these piles and moving them to the right rooms.

Surfaces

The quickest way for a space to look clean is to have a lot of empty space on tables, dresser tops, counters, and the like. Make piles of papers so they don't take up as much room, or better yet grab a shopping bag and throw all the papers in it and toss the thing in the closet and slam the door. It's such a satisfying sound. Once the surfaces are clear, assess their actual filthiness. If they're clear of jelly, you can always use a rag to swipe any remaining detritus onto the floor.

Shiny Stuff

I know it sounds weird, but I learned this from a professional house cleaner. Take a dry paper towel and rub the toothpaste off of your mirror and faucet. Shiny stuff is a giveaway when it's full of gunk. But if shiny stuff actually shines, it creates a force field of seeming tidiness over the rest of a room. Don't ask me how this works, but it's totally official.

Cover Ups

Anything that isn't in a pile or a bag now must go under your bed or in a closet. If your company is going to inspect these places, you must ask yourself if these are really the kind of people you'd like to invite into your home. I mean, if they're going to act like a narcotics team, what's the point?

Warning: You will, at some point in this process, come across a mop, vacuum, or broom. Don't be seduced by the promise of actual cleanliness—you have no time!

Emergencies
If you are really out of time, you may need to:

- Block off an entire section of your house, and confine the mess there. If you have a garage or a basement that you think you can reasonably keep your guests out of without having to act like a serial killer hiding bodies, go ahead and just pile everything in there.

- Or you could close off an area with some plastic sheeting and claim "we're having some work done in there, and it's in quite a state right now."

- Put loose clothing, clean or dirty, in a laundry basket on the back porch. That way it looks as if it might just be waiting to be hung in the fresh breeze.

- Put the dirty dishes into the dryer. Just put a dirty towel under them to catch any wetness. And make a mental note to take them out. (I know a woman whose husband got up the morning after a big party

> and decided start the laundry. Needless to say, she'd forgotten to clue him in on the dishes trick. Good thing it was the pots and pans in there and not Grandma's bone china.) Feng shui principles dictate that you should not have chipped or broken dishes. If any of your dirty dishes are cracked and messing with your energy flow, don't even bother washing them. Feel free to throw them away.

What to do if you are discovered:

It might be hard to explain why the dog is locked in the bathroom with a pile of dirty diapers and the toaster. So when your aunt comes marching out of there (what, she couldn't read the sign that said "occupied"?) and demands to know what is going on, you look her right in the eye and say: Rover has taken a step back in his potty training, but the vet said that every time he goes all by himself like a big dog, he should get a tasty toasted waffle.

In other cases, your best bet might be a redirect. Say your boss's wife is looking down at the cat vomit you missed in the corner of the living room. "Oh, Shirley, look there, out the window. Have you ever seen anything so cute? Could I get you a drink? Or perhaps some beef stroganoff?"

And when you don't have time to take a shower, iron your dress, etc., you might need some party styling.

Your hair is greasy and flat. Bend at the waist and flip your hair upside down. Brush vigorously from the roots to the tips for ten strokes, and flip your hair back up as you come back to standing. Enjoy the head rush, and then look in the mirror. Your hair will be visibly fluffier. You may have to excuse yourself several times to repeat this process throughout the evening.

When nothing you have is clean or when it's all hideously wrinkled:

Go for a sweater. Even if it's been balled up in a corner, you can probably shake it out good and it will look just fine. You can also get dressed and then go stand in the bathroom while you run hot water in the shower and steam yourself a bit.

But beware, party styling is not a long-term solution for lack of personal hygiene. A friend's little sister was in charge of brushing her own hair, and after some time of it seeming to go ok, her mother discovered that she had only ever brushed the top layer, and that the bottom had become pretty much one big gross dreadlock. She had to get a short haircut after that, but it was good while it lasted.

Chapter 4

Excusez-Moi

S'il Vous

PLAIT

Household Excuses

Okay. You are Emily Post incarnate. You are the (subdued) life of the party. You tell hilarious jokes that do not offend anyone. You write heartfelt thank you notes that are in the mail within 24 hours of opening even the most tasteless gift. You arrive on time at social gatherings, have perfect memory for names, and have done your research on pronunciation in many languages. Your attire is suited to every occasion, and you are so prepared and well mannered as to be a rewarding guest as well as an excellent host.

And if you can pull all this off without a stick lodged up your rear, all the better. Bravo. Go on with your big bad self. I am happy to concede that you are a better person than I, and you don't need this chapter. *Move On.*

But if, folks, you are a little (or a lot) messy, forgetful, stingy, tardy, and/or your emotions sometimes get the better of you . . . read on! There really is a good explanation. Well, maybe plausible. Well, an explanation.

If you are reading this book from the start, and I think you really should, you will already have many excuses under your belt for not showing up to social occasions. For those times you can't face going to the six hour baby shower of an office acquaintance (with stupid party games), for times you can't muster the courage to sit through a trip to visit Great Uncle Lucas (whom you and your siblings have always called "Uncle Great Mucous"). You've already got that stuff down pat. Now you need excuses for all manner of social troubles, including your own various states of being.

Also, I think this might be a good time to mention a little trick I like to use. It has happened that even I have been caught off guard in a situation that requires a good excuse. If this happens when I'm on the phone, I thank my lucky stars, because there are some handy dandy little excuses for getting off the phone in a hurry that will at the very least give you time to formulate an effective web of deceit.

"Oh, you need me to rent you a truck and help you move this Saturday?" "Um, ouch! Can I call you back in a minute?" "I just stubbed my toe really bad." OR (ring doorbell here) "There's the door—I'd better get that. Can I buzz ya right back?" OR "Oh my god, I have an eyelash in my eye and it hurts like crazy. Let me get to a mirror and dig it out and I'll call you back." OR (play with the ringtones on your cell phone in the background) "Oh, shoot, that's my [boss, mom] on the other phone. I really have to get that or I'm in big trouble. I'll ring you right back, okay?"

Excuses for Yourself/Your State of Being

Excuse you!

I remember in the seventh grade, walking by Ned Tranton's locker, and someone let out a huge farting noise, pointed at me and said "Excuse YOU!" Hilarity ensued, but I assure you I was not laughing. It was one of the lower points of a generally humiliating year of my life in which I was heavy, gawky, and too good at science to be one of the chosen few.

Anyway, I could've used some good excuses that year—for being an emotional wreck, for not being able to run a mile without puking. Stuff like that. But I digress. Sometimes you need an excuse for your own sorry self. For being tired, psycho, emotional, or giddy. Or on worse days, for being pissy and yelling or throwing things. Or on the worst days, for anti-Semitic rants when you've been pulled over for drunk driving. Actually, there may be no excuse for that last one, but you should still try to make some kind of public statement before five days go by. But I'm not naming any names.

A little rambling can be good.

For these excuses, it might be good to indulge in a bit of rambling: Did I tell you I get a bad reaction to sugar and it just sends me around the bend and that slut behind the counter at One-on-Every-Corner coffee shop told me there was no sugar in the chocolate cupcakes? So it's her fault really that I'm on a sugar binge, and I'm never going back there again except it's really the only place where they make a decent latte. And maybe I can have her fired for obviously lying to me in my vulnerable state when I told her I couldn't do sugar. And then, to top it all off, I think she gave me caffeinated coffee and I was up all night. And did I tell you this is the 15th anniversary of the day I broke up with my first boyfriend?

Or you could just deny your culpability by denying your very existence. I once heard the story of a semifamous writer who lived in New York. (Names have been changed to protect the insane.) An acquaintance spotted her on the street in Berlin in an apparent frothy madness—dressed very strangely and talking to herself—and when this person went up to her and said, "Marie, hi, it's David. Are you ok?" she screamed, "I'm not Marie, god damn it!" and ran away, dragging a lopsided rolling suitcase behind her that was missing one wheel.

You can try telling your boss you took the wrong medication. Tylenol 3 has Codeine in it and it looks a lot like vitamins.

Maybe you took the wrong medication. Tylenol 3 is the one with codeine in it, and apparently it looks very much like some vitamins. So what if you pulled an all-nighter so you could stay up and watch the back-to-back marathons of *Friday the Thirteenth* and *Nightmare on Elm Street*? (I love October.) Nobody has to know that's why you're so tired you can't function—just tell them you popped some codeine by accident. This happens all the time. It even happens in hospitals all the time, but I don't know if we should go into it here, because it could make me start to feel very paranoid. But maybe doctors should have some better excuse than their lame handwriting for messing up approximately who knows and who cares how many prescriptions every year.

Mariah Carey was hospitalized for "exhaustion" a while back and explained, "All I needed was, like, five hours' sleep." Dude, Mariah, I totally hear ya. That was definitely not, like, a drug problem or a psychotic break or anything. A girl needs her beauty rest. And beauty rest isn't really beauty rest until you've got some kind of IV drip with a nice sedative mixed in.

Inappropriate attire

When I used to temp (I say that like I haven't done it in years, but I really did it last week. What, you think writing a book is like winning the lotto or something?). Anyway, when I used to temp I was always trying to jerry-rig an acceptable outfit. It seemed ridiculous to use a week's worth of temp pay to go out and buy a suit, so I worked out every combination possible of slacks plus tank tops under decent-looking sweaters. Once I swear I could not find a pair of shoes that matched, except for some strappy sandals from my cousin's wedding last year, and I knew the policy was no open-toed shoes. But I really had no choice. So I used some first aid tape and taped together my two small toes, and told everyone I could that I had broken my pinky toe chasing after my sister's kid who was unraveling toilet paper through the entire house. Nobody bothered about the shoes, and I got kudos for babysitting and tons of sympathy for being a gimp.

And, as we know, celebrities outdo us plebes in every way. But they don't usually bother making excuses for the ridiculous stuff that passes for runway attire these days. They just parade around with their nipples popping out. Or worse. I heard on some gossip show that a particular socialite/singer/novelist/porn star was photographed showing her lady parts as she got out of her car. Her excuse for not wearing any underwear? "I was. It was transparent."

Clumsy?

Maybe you're like me—covered in mystery bruises from constantly running into corners and countertops. I graduated from high school in a cast because I broke my foot *stepping off a curb*. The only Spanish I remember from taking three years of it was from the section on irregular verbs: "Caigo con frecuencia porque soy muy torpe." Translation: I fall a lot because I'm very clumsy.

Reporting in the October 2006 issue of the journal *Archives of Pediatrics & Adolescent Medicine*, researchers at Columbia University Medical Center in New York City conducted intelligence and motor-skills tests on 474 nondisabled teens, average age 16, who weighed less than 2,000 grams (4.5 pounds) at birth. The results showed that these teens had more motor-skills problems than other teens.

Another good one for sympathy points: "I fall a lot because I'm very clumsy."

So, really, only your mother will know that you were not a preemie. And now you have a study to cite the next time you drop a platter of food at your restaurant job, or step on the foot of a burly gentleman with neck tattoos on the subway.

Forgetting

When she can't remember the name of the novel she's recommending to me, or when she forgets the name of the cat we had when I was little, or can't find her car in the parking lot, my mom likes to say that she's having a "senior moment." Okay. I would like to go on the record and say these are total crap. Because I have them all the time and I'm twenty nine. Well, thirty. Thirty-ish. I think. And in dog years that's 210. What were we saying?

Instead of senior moments, you might go with something else that can lead to short-term memory loss (besides drug use, my hippie friends):

Chronic Fatigue Syndrome. This is one of my favorites for missing work, too. And I just found out it can also lead to loss of memory.

Concussion. Bump your head hard enough, and you might be able to forget all your exes. Somebody get me a rubber mallet.

Amnesic shellfish poisoning. Though very rare, some people get a reaction to eating shrimp where they have permanent short-term memory loss. I wonder if they forget that they can't eat shellfish anymore, or if they have to get some sort of med-alert bracelet to warn waitresses and fishmongers.

Being a woman. Did you know that pregnancy can make you forget stuff? Well, I guess that's nature's way of preparing you to slouch off the pain of childbirth and get on with overpopulating the planet. And count forgetfulness among the many annoying and ongoing symptoms of menopause. I mean, couldn't they have cut us ladies a break?

Forgetting names—a proactive approach

You know this moment of terror, when you see someone, and maybe they're someone you've known casu-
ally for many years—like a neighbor, or someone from
church—and you don't have one single clue what their
name is. Couldn't guess the first letter. Here are a few
strategies for how to deal with this embarrassing
moment so they'll never guess you forgot!

If you are with someone else, you can always try saying "you guys know each other, right?" And then pretend
you see something really interesting across the street
for a quick moment while you leave them to introduce
themselves. But you must not actually get absorbed in
something across the street and miss hearing the forgotten moniker, or everything will be for naught.

If you're with someone else you can also introduce
that person. "How are you, have you met my husband,
BLANK?" This leaves them to say their name. This must
be done with utter confidence. No stammering. No
pausing, or they may be on to you.

If you are by yourself, you must take it upon yourself
to bluff your way through it. If the occasion arises and
the conversation gets around to it, you could offer to
send this person the article you've just been discussing
by email. When you get the email address it will

hopefully be something obvious like "addiejohnson @bigexcuses.com." But if not, never fear—hopefully they will write you back and include a signature with all their pertinent info.

And if it comes down to it, there is a kind of aphasia that you can get after a stroke (even a mild one) or sometimes for other reasons like getting hit on the head where you forget how to recognize people's faces. So when you don't recognize someone or you forget their name and you pretend you don't recognize them, you can very sincerely blush and describe your condition.

In any case, you must resist the temptation to use annoying nicknames. "Hey, baby," "Hi honey," or "Ahoy there, matey" will just make you sound like the big fat idiot that you in fact are.

Forgetting birthdays or other important dates

If you don't get a birthday present for your mother, you're in deep doo-doo. And maybe you have a really good reason. But chances are, no matter how good your reason sounds to you, your mother is maybe not going to agree that your reason is *a really good reason*. In fact she may think it is a lame-ass excuse. Even if it's not.

But don't whine about it. This case calls for a good excuse that also puts you on the right track for making it up to her big-time. Which is what you should do. Because she's your mom. She pushed you out of her hoo-hah, for god's sake. It's the least you can do. I suggest calling her up and explaining that you don't have her present yet because you're having it made. This buys you a couple of months but it also puts the onus on you to get her something really good that falls under the category of "being made" or making something really amazing your-self and passing it off as the work of a local artisan. Your karma will be restored and you'll have a happy mama.

There are no good excuses for forgetting your anniversary. Just forget it pal, and be prepared to spend the big bucks on the fancy, making-it-all-up-to-her vacation.

For most family members' and friends' birthdays, it will suffice to say your bag was stolen with your calen-dar/handheld device/etc. in it, and you're so sorry you forgot. They've probably forgotten yours for most of your life anyway, so hopefully it won't be too big a deal. My father forgot his own birthday once. Therefore, I feel if I ever forget his birthday in the future I have the perfect excuse—if he did it, why can't I?

If you forget your anniversary, you are in trouble. I'm generalizing here, but usually it's the guys who are forgetting and the ladies who are remembering and get *really pissed* when you forget. I think the best way to get out of the doghouse on this one is to fake a big old surprise. You will have to do some quick thinking and spend some major cash, but let me tell you it will pay back dividends. Book a last minute, all-inclusive weekend away. If you have a really nosy spouse, do it in cash at a travel agency or have a friend do it so that she can't look at the credit card statement and see you booked it the day after the big day. And then go drink fruity concoctions with umbrellas in them on the beach and have sex and all the rest of it, and I think she should be able to get over it. And I have yet to meet a man (other than my husband, I swear) who instinctively understands the amnesiatic and aphrodisiac effects of jewelry. 'Nuff said.

When you do something really stupid or embarassing, sometimes the best plan is to skip the excuses and go for the truth.

Stupid stuff that embarrasses yourself and others

For shouting "hi" to someone you don't know, for introducing yourself to a tree, for putting your big foot in your big mouth, for getting too drunk and acting like an ass, for not being able to pay your part of the bill, for showing up to work or school with a black eye. You'd better have something to say the next day. In these cases, I would go for a nice convoluted sob story. Or you could always *gasp* tell the truth. Or some version of the truth.

A friend in college told me he woke up with a black eye and was fuzzy on the details of how he got it, so he told his boss he stepped in to stop some guy in a club from beating up his girlfriend, and was later jumped by the guy's pals. The boss bought it and word of his valor spread through the office.

I got a black eye once from walking into a door. Seriously. See above section about being clumsy. But other ways to get a black eye? Playing with a dog and bonking heads, building a porch for your grandmother and getting smacked with a 2x4, getting elbowed during a basketball game.

I have never done this personally, but I know it happens that people get intoxicated and do and say things they wish they hadn't. Some perfectly good reasons for getting sozzled include: I'm poor and there was an open bar. I didn't eat anything beforehand. The ladies I lunch with had a three-martini blow-out in honor of my promotion, and who am I to turn down a toast?

Now, you also have the option here of telling the truth, in a very sober, apologetic kind of way. You can admit you have a problem and need help. Sometimes this works. I mean, who are they going to blame, Johnny Walker? Then again, sometimes it backfires, as when you take five days to issue a public apology about your embarrassing drunk driving arrest in Malibu. But when this unnamed star got to some real truthiness that starts like this:

"There is no excuse, nor should there be any tolerance, for anyone who thinks or expresses any kind of anti-Semitic remark."

And ends like this

"It's about existing in harmony in a world that seems to have gone mad."

You have to give him some props for not really taking the blame at all. This is a mad world, and we understand that's what drove him to speed at 87 mph down the Pacific Coast Highway. And it was probably some rabbi who tossed the open bottle of tequila in the car. So sneaky, those religious sages.

Not picking up the tab

This can be an awkward thing at the end of a dinner date, when the little black tray comes and any two enlightened, modern individuals are totally clueless about what should happen next. Men don't want to seem chauvinistic, women don't want to be dependent, and if you're gay, fuggedaboudit. And then there are times you really don't want to go dutch, or worse, you can't. Maybe you assumed your aunt was treating on her trip to town, but she's all set to teach you a lesson about budgeting. Well, you'll show her.

If it's one of those places where they don't want to rush you, so you have to very specifically ask for the check. You can get up after the meal and excuse yourself to the bathroom, and request the check on your way. With any luck, there will be a shiny credit card on that little platter when you get back from the loo, and all will be well.

If not, start to dig around in your purse or coat pockets, and then dig more frantically as you "realize" you've forgotten your wallet. I have a friend who can blush on cue. She just has to think about some traumatic embarrassment from her childhood, and then she lights up with shiny pink cheeks. You are mortified, you are so sorry, you must have left it in your other purse/jacket/pants. Oh my god, can I pay you back? If there is even a touch of Sarah Bernhardt in your performance, I guarantee the other party will happily pay the bill without realistically expecting anything in return (if only to stop the gush of tears they sense might be on the way). You can then explain that you walked out of the house with nothing but your bus pass. For good measure, you might ask to use their cell phone to call your roommate to let you in later. Hey, keep going in this vein and you might picket an extra $20 for cab fare.

If you have been dining with someone you would like to remain friendly or romantic with, I do suggest calling the next day and offering to make it up to them. Make plans for the day after your paycheck posts, and you're in business!

Chapter 5

Delivery

FAILURE

Subsystem

Mailboxes, Messages, Missives
Gone Awry, Oh My!

In this modern world, everything should be easier. We have the ability to reach out and touch anyone by shooting missives through the air, the wires, into space satellites, or however it all freaking gets there, and this is supposed to make our lives better. The annoying thing is that when you had to type them on a manual typewriter or write them out longhand, you couldn't be expected to write more than a couple of letters a week for any reason. Now, because email and voicemail make communication so "easy," it is not unheard of to receive 150 emails a day and be expected to respond to at least half of them. *What?!* At 163 average words per email, and 50 emails a day, and typing at 40 wpm, you are still spending a staggering 204 minutes (that's over 3½ *hours*) every day communicating by email.

This does not include time spent on the phone, listening to endless voicemail messages from your BFF or your coworkers. And the worst part is you are mostly chattering about inane crap that people would decide for themselves if they knew they couldn't get ahold of you to go back and forth fifteen times with. And there is the aha! moment. Make yourself *unavailable* and you take yourself out of the vicious cycle of inanity and ridiculous redundancy. Make it seem like the technical elements of your life have a vicious vendetta

If you are a technophobe, you've got a plethora of excuses at your fingertips.

and are out for your blood, and who can blame you for not getting back to them in time?

General Excuses for Communication Breakdowns

I once had a boss who called me the "fax witch." He said it in the nicest possible way, and all it meant was that I was able to troubleshoot the fax machine on the frequent occasions it went kaput. There wasn't much to it, but he was convinced it took a bit of magic and nerves of steel to face that monster. I got the feeling that he truly believed that if he checked the power cord it might turn into a writhing snake, and that if he cracked open the cover to check the ink supply, well, molten lava might shoot out onto his face. If you are this kind of technophobe, you clearly have a plethora of great excuses at your fingertips.

Germ phobia might justify calling in sick, especially in winter. Or, people migh just think you're weird.

If you also harbor even a slight germ phobia, I would like to share with you this factoid I just learned: a desk has 400 times more bacteria per square inch than a toilet seat. And a telephone? Even more. This to me is a totally valid reason not to pick up the phone or touch a keyboard for days at a time. In fact, it might even justify calling in sick.

Keeping in touch with our parents and grandparents

Sometimes we need to make it clear to the people who donated our genetic material and/or raised us (a.k.a. our parents) that the umbilical cord has been severed and that the nest is a barren wasteland. I don't have this problem, as my mother was turning my bedroom into an office within twenty minutes of me leaving for my first semester at college, and sounded a bit offended when I said I'd see her at Christmas.

But I have watched friends as they painfully shut off their cell phones, or erase unanswered voicemails asking if they had remembered to take out their contact lenses and take their asthma inhaler with them. These friends, in their middle thirties, have had enough. And I don't blame them. Now, don't be mean, but it's okay to make a lame excuse to your mom for not calling her back. In fact, I think it sort of drives home the point. Like, "Oh, yeah, mom, sorry I didn't call you back all week. There was a really big test in badminton class and I had to study."

Or, "I have a big presentation for the investors at work on Monday and my doctor put me on vocal rest."

Do me a favor though, if the messages get to a hysteric pitch and it's clear your mother is imagining you pinned under a train, just call her back. I don't want to be held responsible for any heart attacks. In fact, I don't want to be held responsible for anything—that's why I wrote this book.

A note on "get right back to me"

Different people have very different ideas about the acceptable amount of elapsed time that can pass after leaving a message before it becomes rude that you haven't responded yet. I say three to five days is downright speedy. I take as my guide the fact that my voicemail automatically deletes saved messages after one month. A month. So as long as I call back before 30 days are up, I feel fine. But you make the call.

And this is a pet peeve of mine. When you're at work and someone sends an email that notifies the sender as soon as it is opened, I call this the tattle-tale email. How passive-aggressive. How rude. Can't I just read my emails in my own sweet time and really take some time to formulate my response? It just takes all the fun out of the delayed response. Hardly gives you time to think of a something witty to shoot back before you're in the doghouse for being lazy, or worse, you might actually have to stop surfing the Internet and work a little.

Things Not Working as They Should

It is your job to train your boss—and also your family, or anyone else you might not want to talk to with the frequency they'd like you to. This may not be easy (excuses are hard work, people). You may have to do everything short of getting one of those clicker things they use to reward dogs when they do something right. I bet your boss would really like one of those.

Train them all to know that you are never reliably reachable in any medium. Not by email, not by phone, or instant message, or carrier pigeon. If your boss is in the habit of wandering over to your desk to communicate his or her needs, you must get in the habit of going to the bathroom a lot. Or to the filing cabinets, or the copy machine, or down to the messenger center. Eventually your boss will learn not to depend on you and will begin to complete his or her own tasks.

Some of our toys of modern technology—email (server down), cell phone (in a no-service area)—can make great excuses.

Imagine the sense of accomplishment and independence he/she will feel. Really, you're doing good works here.

For a long time, our computer at home was really, really old so there eventually came a time when it got too old to communicate with any of the new fancy websites on the internet, including our free email program. The website would shut down the computer, making it impossible to read or send more than one email at a time. Believe me, this was great excuse fodder for a long time and included lots of trips to the computer repair shop and long drawn-out phone calls to technical support.

And this stuff hardly needs to be faked. We all know that modern technology doesn't always function as it should. And some of the features of modern technology can be blamed to great effect, even when they do work as they should.

Your Bulk Mail Folder

Yes, this is the place to go for all those pesky emails about home loans and enlargements of various parts of your anatomy and such, but because no system is perfect, occasionally an important email slips through the cracks and ends up there. And even if it doesn't, who's the wiser?

Voicemail

I don't know about you, but for some reason half the time people call us it says that our mailbox is full, even when it isn't. This is clearly a problem that needs fixing, but every time my husband sits down to call the phone company and embarks on a 34-minute wait time, he begins to rethink the value of voicemail altogether. Eventually he gives up, and we trade the inconvenience of being unreachable for the relief of not having to return so many phone calls.

Cell Phones

These things are the paragon of modern (in)convenience. They lose service, they drop calls, you go over your minutes and have a strict budget that won't allow paying 75 cents a minute, and to top it all off you actually have to remember to plug the thing in every night before going to bed or you can't be reached at all the next day. What a shame. But wait, there's more! Your cell phone could:

- Fall from jacket pocket into foul toilet bowl in a seedy bar.

- Be thrown into oncoming traffic because it cut me off three times in the middle of a knock-down drag-out with a very important person.

- Have gone overboard while fishing.

- Have a jammed 5 key.

- Be stuck on tetris, so all you can do is try to beat your high score in the hopes that that will kick it back to normal.

Every city that I've been in seems to have a Bermuda triangle inside the confines of which there is no hope of making any calls or checking any messages. Maybe you have an "all day meeting" in the center of this spot?

Email Subsystem Failure

OK, so maybe you just typed the email address wrong, but it sounds much more fancy and official to say "it's so strange, the email I sent you got bounced back to me as 'undeliverable' due to 'permanent fatal errors.' That sounded so scary I just gave up."

The Mail

Yes, we still depend on this good old workhorse. And yes, sometimes it still fails us. Or doesn't, and we can pretend it did. Have you ever gotten one of those plastic bags from the post office with a mashed-up letter inside? It has a little note from the postmaster general saying so sorry to have mangled your missive, etc., etc. Well, why not stow the bag in a drawer so if you ever need to pretend you didn't get an important piece of mail you can douse it with orange juice and shred the edges and pop it in there, and no one will be the wiser.

Chapter 6

GET

Out

OF IT

Crimes and Misdemeanors and Other Crap

I **hate it when people say they want to be a kid again. Or comment how great it looks to be pushed around in a stroller like a baby. They** conveniently forget that babies can't talk or go where they want to go, and they have to wait for someone to clean up the mess in their pants. The least we can do is roll them down the block in some kind of comfort. And that nostalgia some people have for being in high school again? Whew, no thanks.

But there are certain things about being a grownup that really stink. Like going to the dentist, paying bills and parking tickets, or having to show up in court when you do something really stupid. So while I don't advocate a return to diapers, I say get out of it all in style and be an adult, but with none of the fuss! And hope it doesn't catch up with you anytime soon.

Adult Life Excuses—not getting a job, living with your parents, losing stuff, late papers and presentations/reports

A Job? I Don't Need No Stinkin' Job

I'm too busy to get a job. I mean, I'm waiting for the right position to come along. Okay, I'll be honest. Nobody wants to hire me. Maybe you could move to another country—I hear Spain is nice, and their unemployment rate hovers around 20%, which means you really probably can't get a job. And a friend of mine who was just there said that all the museums have unemployment rates for admission that are even less than those for students and seniors. Score.

And if you don't have a job, it's hard to find a place to live. So you'll also need an excuse for still living with your parents. In Italy, it's very common for children, mostly young men, to live with their parents well into their thirties. If you have any bit of Italian heritage, I encourage you to use this ploy on your mother. Imagine the savings on rent and food.

Losing Stuff

Kids lose stuff all the time. It's a given and it's generally forgiven. I left a flute on a public bus once when I was nine, and there was a big hullabaloo while my dad called the bus company and thankfully we tracked it down. But nobody was too annoyed with me (well, after a couple of days anyway). In my adult life, I have lost fewer than 20 but more than twelve cell phones (I'm totally not exaggerating) and, yes, it has happened that I have misplaced half of a pair of shoes I was wearing. That would be one shoe. Gone forever, and no leads, and no clues left behind. I could not explain it to my mother, and I cannot explain it now beyond an abstract theory of a transient dead zone. Unfortunately, there is not so much cutting of slack as there used to be in my youth.

As we get older, we also have more stuff, and more important stuff, that we shouldn't be losing. I cannot, for the life of me, remember passwords. I take the advice to heart that it should be something semi-obscure but still memorable, and in the moment of creating it I feel certain I will not forget. How could I forget muffin1410? That's my first cat's name and my first address. Simple. Sure. I sometimes even write it down on a little slip of paper, and then put the paper "someplace safe." Unfortunately, "someplace safe" in my life just means "never again accessible on this plane of reality."

In school, when a paper was late you lost points. Maybe even a whole grade. But this possibility could always be measured up against how much fun you could be having not writing the paper this weekend, but instead partying like a fool for 48 hours and turning it in a day late for a lesser grade on Tuesday. In the adult world, the punctuality of projects and presentations is closely tied to things like job performance, promotions, and raises, and even whether or not you get fired. Yeesh, that cuts too close to the bone for me. If you do have a late project, and there is no obvious third party to pin the blame on, you need to do some creative detective work. By this I mean detective work where you are actually creating the clues before you are discovering them. It spoils the "aha!" moment a bit, but it's still totally worth it, I promise.

If you do have a late project, and there is no obvious third party to pin the blame on, you need to do some creative detective work.

Go through the process in your head piece by piece and find as many "unforeseen problems" as possible. Maybe you didn't get a delivery on time, maybe the graphics took longer to print than they told you, maybe a key member of your team had a computer tragedy and was up all night with technical support, but lost the better part of the work up to that point.

These things should be at least partly linked to the truth, so that you can back up your assertions with "proof." And if you are asked why you didn't share this information until the due date? You may reply, with a hangdog look, that you and your team were earnestly trying to work to make up for the delay, and thought (yes, perhaps too optimistically) that you could pull it off in time. You are so sorry, and you only need X amount of time and Y amount of money to finish off the job right.

Finances

Agh! Nobody told me that probably the worst part of being an adult was that I would have to deal with money every day of my life. What happened to my allowance, with its simple equation of chores to dollars? No taxes taken out, no bills to pay, no concerns about investments or inflation. I have been on the bad side of the phone company more times than I can say, and have learned a thing or two about (not) paying bills.

The basic excuses are often just fine—your roommate moved out and took all the mail with her. Your statement is incorrect and you need an adjusted bill sent to you via the slowest possible post. You've been out of town for three months (working on a film, caring for your sick grandfather) and had your mail held at the post office, and you just picked it up today.

You can just claim that you never received a copy of your statement and ask for a new one. Did you know (and I probably shouldn't tell you this because now you'll never even make the effort to pay on time) that if you're going to be late on a bill and you call and tell them, they're actually usually really cool about it? Often you don't even need a good excuse, although I like to throw one in for good measure and to spice up the life of the person who has to sit fielding calls from other broke slackers all day.

I once told a bill collector that I needed more time to pay because my husband always took care of all the bills but he had just left with another woman. The drone on the phone stammered how sorry he was and said he'd make a note in the account and to get it paid up as soon as possible, but he understood I was going through a difficult time. He was very supportive, particularly for a bill collector. I did not mention that the other woman my husband walked out the door with happened to be his mother, and left out the detail that they were on their way to the grocery store.

Somebody also told me once, and don't hate me for this if it's not true because I'm not actually organized enough to try it, but if you don't pay on time and somebody puts a bad note on your credit report, you can write letters to the credit bureaus saying that you are contesting the charge and would like the item removed from your report. Then the company has to respond and blah blah blah, and the long and the short is that those big companies are not generally organized enough to actually respond in the given time frame, so the credit bureaus will usually remove the item.

If you don't want to talk to a telemarketer, you can try telling them you're dead.

You could try being dead. A friend's teenaged daughter answered the phone while I was at their house once. After listening to the beginnings of a pitch about a valuable timeshare opportunity, she told the phone solicitor that her father was dead, and would not be needing any vacation homes. We were gobsmacked. But it worked, and luckily her father didn't mind being nixed in name for the sake of a little peace from those crazy phone people.

Death and . . .

Speaking of death, I'm thinking of the other inevitable thing in this life. You know it—taxes.

Taxes are the sort of thing that, once you start not filing them, become increasingly difficult and start to take on their own status as uber excuse. You worry about getting them in on time, and then one year you file an extension, and let me tell you from there it's a slippery slope to just not filing for 17 years. And then you're into it with the IRS, and they want to settle, and there are lawyers and all that. And then you need to take some time off work, and you're exempt from housecleaning or doing any favors for maiden aunts, because those are the least of your problems.

There are things that become excuses for themselves through sheer neglectfulness. If 3 years worth of unfiled taxes is enough to threaten to send you for a short to medium length stay at your local psych ward, Is it really worth it?

This is why people tell you not to get behind on stuff like this. Same goes for the dentist. These are things that become excuses for themselves through sheer neglect-fulness. They pile up and become such a monster of hor-ribleness in your psyche that even beginning to think about how you are going to tackle 3 years worth of unfiled taxes is enough to threaten to send you for a short to medium length stay at your local psych ward, which would really have a negative effect on so many other things and people in your life, is it really worth it? And if the fillings aren't actually falling out of your mouth during a job interview or something, what's the point in going to the dentist to hear that you have to come back every week for the next two months while they do major road construction in your mouth, and that you'll pay a small fortune for the privilege. It's not that bad. Don't tell me. Denial ain't just a river in Egypt.

Parking Tickets, Jury Duty, and Other Civic Annoyances

Parking, Speeding, and Other Tickets

My friend Polly has an uncle who explained to a police officer that he was speeding because his wife was in labor. The cop said, "Yeah, right." And her uncle replied, "Just look in the back seat." And there she was, so they gave them a police escort to the hospital.

If you are not lucky enough to have so convincing an excuse, you must take it upon yourself to get away with it by sheer wit and innovation. First, you can ask them for proof you were speeding, because apparently they haven't always got it. But if they do, now they're probably pretty annoyed with your smartass self, so you'll maybe just have to take the ticket. It's okay—you can fight it later in court.

I hear tell that if you actually show up to fight almost any ticket, you usually win, because the cop who caught you can't spend all day hanging around in court.

You can reuse any number of gross excuses from earlier chapters, including symptoms of diarrhea and nausea as good excuses for speeding to the nearest toilet. Also, even in the early stages of pregnancy (before your start to show) the need to pee can be overwhelming.

If you do get nailed, I hear tell that if you actually show up to fight almost any ticket, you usually win, because the cop who caught you can't spend all day hanging around in court, there are other scofflaws besides yourself out there to catch. Now, I'm not saying it's a whole lot of fun to spend your day downtown waiting for your number to be called in traffic court, but consider the possibility that if you tell your story of wrongful ticketing (with choice embellishments, of course) to your boss, you'll probably get the whole day off from work to go down there. And you're probably out after a couple of hours and have the rest of the day all to yourself! Even if you have the sort of boss you don't think will be forgiving about the time off, don't you dare waste a personal day on this one—see Chapter 1—and call in a sickie!

Jury Duty

I have always been that person who does not hold up my end of the bargain in this department. I know, I know, it is a responsibility of citizenship. But I am not alone on this—who sees that distinctive piece of mail in their box and sings with glee? I always request a postponement as many times as the law allows, and then when I really have to go in, I formulate my plan.

They can't make you serve if it's going to be a financial hardship for you or if you have a good medical excuse. If you are working for a temp agency or in some other week-to-week situation and can prove that you are not being remunerated for missing a day or a week of work, they will excuse you, as that comes under the financial hardship category. If you have a friend who's a doctor, they can probably write you some kind of note.

But the best thing is to not get chosen or get dismissed from a jury—that way they can't call you again for a few years, and by that time maybe you'll have moved to Spain and be enjoying the unemployment rates around town.

There are a lot of crazy citizens out there, and who will be the wiser if you join their ranks on the day your number is called?

How do you avoid being chosen for a jury? There are a lot of crazy citizens out there, and who will be the wiser if you join their ranks on the day your number is called? Show a bias for whatever issue is on the table. If it's about gang violence, state your clear contention that gangs are just harmless social groups, or that gang members deserve whatever they get. Or you could tell the prosecutor that you think police brutality is the biggest problem in the justice system. If you are familiar enough with it, quote the Bible. Talk about Jesus incessantly. It might leave people uneasy enough to move on to the guy to your left. You could also state your extreme feelings about the death penalty, either way. Especially if it's a case of shoplifting, or a civil suit, and has nothing to do with the death penalty. And if you can shed real tears at any point in the questioning, please do.

The last time I did jury duty, there was a pregnant woman who said she couldn't serve during questioning. She went into far too much detail about how long she had tried to become pregnant and that it was a difficult pregnancy, and that she didn't want to expose herself and her baby to any undue stress or violent images. She said she feared going into early labor right there in the courtroom. She really went on and on, but nobody stopped her because it seemed like a heartfelt speech. By the end of it, all of us including the judge and the stenographer were happy to see her go.

Crimes and Misdemeanors

I never understood that phrase—aren't misdemeanors also crimes? I guess they're less serious crimes, so I guess it's like saying crimes and sort-of crimes.

If you have committed a crime, or are accused of a crime you did not commit, you will have to come up with some kind of explanation. Famous people are really good at this, and they usually get off easy. Unless they're Martha Stewart.

Saks Fifth Avenue guard Colleen Rainey testified during Winona Ryder's shoplifting trial that the actress had explained she was preparing for a movie role and, "I was told that I should shoplift. The director said I should try it out."

Paris Hilton's excuse for falling on her face during a sobriety test after being pulled over for driving erratically? "It was nothing. I'd been shooting my music video for my new song, I got off last night at about 10 p.m. I had dinner with my sister and all my girlfriends, and then we went to this charity event Dave Navarro threw for brain tumors. I had one margarita. I was starving 'cause I had not ate all day. I was on my way to In-N-Out which is probably three blocks away because I was just really hungry and I wanted an In-N-Out burger!" Whoa, Paris, keep to the story there—remember your lies! And fix your grammar! You had dinner after ten but hadn't "ate" all day?

Then, there are those doping scandals. I think an excuse is really top notch when you can involve a conspiracy theory that goes all the way to the hairy, ugly top. Like the high jumper Javier Sotomayor, 1992

Olympic champion. When he came up positive for cocaine he said he was the victim of an elaborate conspiracy by the American CIA, who "may have put some substance in his lunch or dinner." Cuban sports officials and the Cuban government had his back, and a vice president of the Cuban Council of Ministers said "What is the hairy, ugly, powerful hand behind this? We do not know yet. . . . Certain agencies can do anything, even things we can't think of."

I think an excuse is really top notch when you can involve a conspiracy theory that goes all the way to the hairy, ugly top.

Stranger things have happened. Did you hear about the guy in Nigeria who was accused of murdering his own brother with an axe? He said he was chasing away some stray goats who were hanging around on his farm, and when one wouldn't leave, he attacked it with an axe. That's when the goat turned back into his brother.

"All I know is, I woke up and I am covered in cream," says Peter Buck, of R.E.M. He was acquitted of turning over a breakfast cart during an air-rage rampage. But he said he blacked out because he took a sleeping pill on an empty stomach (along with a few drinks).

Don't use any excuse that has "rage" anywhere in it. Like "sports rage" or "road rage." Don't say you were mentally unstable and you ate too many Twinkies and drank too much Coca Cola and therefore you're not liable for your actions. Think of something better. Where am I going with this? Find a sense of humor. Be innovative. If you must use rage as your excuse, claim you had "floral rage," in which the floral arrangements that were sent to you as opening night gifts were so pungent that you actually went insane,

Don't use any excuse that has "rage" anywhere in it. If you must use rage as your excuse, claim you had "floral rage."

and you can't remember why you peed on the subway tracks after downing 8 or 9 martinis. The martinis themselves were most certainly not the cause. It was those lilies, man—a heady brew.

These six words may sound like the answer to your prayers: "Not guilty by reason of insanity." But yo, tread lightly with the insanity excuses. And keep in mind, it won't work in Montana, Idaho, or Utah—they don't even recognize this as a legitimate excuse! Besides, even if you are found to have been a nut job on the date and time in question, you'll still probably be doing your time in some state mental ward, and I hear those places are no fun, no fun at all.

Chapter 7

I'd

Love to,

BUT...

"**The** boy who is good at excuses is generally good for nothing else," said Samuel Foote. Well, duh, why do you think he has to make all those excuses in the first place? We could all do well to take a cue from this boy. He is good at nothing, and therefore he has a great excuse for everything. This chapter is about incompetence—mine, yours, someone else's. And it's about showing your excuse through action, rather than just blurting it out and hoping it works. These are, in my opinion, the most convincing excuses.

Excuse Clinic

I got on a plane once with two carry-on bags and a sleeping infant. As I got to my seat, I hoped the flight attendant would help me put one bag in the overhead compartment. He suddenly made himself very busy at the coffee machine in the back. When I finally tracked him down and asked for his help he snipped, "Oh no, uh-uh, I'm under doctors orders—no heavy lifting for me." I glared at him, and luckily an elderly gentleman came to my rescue (though a 70-year-old man lifting a heavy bag over his head is not my idea of a happy ending). If

The most convincing excuses often come through action.

the attendant had wanted an even better excuse, he could have bent down to get the bag and then cried out in pain as he tried to lift the bag and then dropped it on the floor, faking a stubbed toe in the process. This would be showing, not telling. And instead of being so pissed that a flight attendant couldn't perform a basic function of his job and was way sassy about it, I might have had real sympathy for the guy and his back injury. Such a wasted opportunity on his part.

And then there are those comments I like to call excuses plus! These are little add-ons tacked on the back of a good excuse. Like, "I'm so sorry I can't help you scrapbook your trip to Africa to help the orphans. Last time I tried to do anything like that I sliced open my finger and bled all over my sister's wedding album." Add on: "But if you need it I have a whole box of unused glue and stickers you can have." Your lame excuse is redirected in a positive direction, outside of your area of responsibility or expertise. The whole idea is to remove yourself as far away from any responsibility as possible.

I'm Not Good at That . . . And Other Reasons I Just Can't

Don't say *won't*, say *can't*.

Say you won't do something, and you're asking for trouble. I won't eat my peas! I won't take out the trash! Say that and you're just spoiling for a fight. Won't implies defiance, selfishness, even outright tyranny. But can't? Ah, can't. Hard to argue with incompetence, hard to belittle helplessness, hard to come down hard on dejected failure. For every task you feel confident doing there are thousands of others that are clearly beyond your reach. And kudos to you if it's one of those get-up-and-go days when you're willing to try and fail and try again. But if it's not, count on *can't*.

Donald Trump can't change a diaper. This, from one of the most financially successful men in the world. "I would never ask to change him," Trump told the *New York Post*. "Melania probably wouldn't let me. I'd just do it wrong." We hear ya.

When someone asks me to do something, I often pretend that it entails far more than I could possible accomplish. I honed this skill when I was a teenager and my parents insisted I clean my room (where you rarely caught a glimpse of the floor underneath my piles of papers and clothes). I had a ready

Never say won't, say can't.

answer. I'd love to clean my room, but I can't. I have to leave for rehearsal in an hour and a half, and if I pick up all the dirty clothes, I'll have to put them in the washer, and if they sit in the washer while I'm gone I'll forget so by the time I get back I'll just go to bed and then three days later when I remember they'll probably be growing mold from sitting wet in the washer. And I don't have my filing system in place yet, so if I move the papers from where they are I'll never actually be able to find the research that I need for my history report that's due on Friday and besides I think the cat just had kittens in my closet, and it would be inhumane to try to move them all now at this precious moment in the cycle of their bonding process. And usually part way through they would give up and agree that as long as I confined the mess to my own room and they could shut the door, it was fine for now.

If you're looking for an "I can't" excuse, feel free to go through any of the other chapters in this book for some great situations you might find yourself in to bolster your inability to do just about anything. Need a good excuse to go out to dinner? Well, you can't cook. Your mother never taught you so you're self taught, which means it's 50/50 it'll even be edible, and if it is there are all those dishes to do afterward and did I tell you about my grandmother slicing a tendon while doing dishes? I have a phobia. It's just not going to happen. But I know a great sushi place down the block.

Calling attention to how busy you are with altruistic tasks is often a very successful excuse.

You will also find there are plenty of states of being that will prevent you from doing whatever onerous task is at hand. Maybe you're just too young and inexperienced. Then again, you might be too old for this crap and your knees are already kaput. Can't focus at work because it's the dead of winter and you're depressed, or maybe it's spring and you're too excited to be outside and you just can't pay attention. There's spring fever, and if that doesn't work there's the more scientific hay fever.

Runny nose, blocked sinuses, headache, scratchy throat—who can get anything done with all that going on?

I'm Too Good at It

I'm such a paragon of virtue and industry that I couldn't possibly take anything else on at this moment. Or later, either, to be frank.

Are you a can-do kind of person? Resourceful, energetic, determined? Wow, just writing those three words tired me out—I think I have to go take a nap. I'm three weeks past deadline on this book and I'm running out of credible excuses, but the best one I've used lately is what a busy, virtuous person I really am. I've been doing so much good for others and for the world that I haven't been able to squeeze in any time for writing.

First, I had a friend get sick and pass it to her daughter, who had to be picked up from day care with a bad case of diarrhea. Well, my friend couldn't get out of work 'cause she already used all her sick days, and I'm the emergency contact so I trooped up there in the rain and hauled this poopy kid home to put her in the tub. She's doing much better now, but then I remembered I had signed up to plaster the neighborhood with signage for the upcoming election, and also to get out and register voters after my shift at the soup kitchen. And on top of that, my elderly neighbor Edna broke her hip, and her son broke his arm falling on the ice while he was trying to get her into the car, so I sat with the two of them in the emergency room for six hours on Friday, which cut into the time I was supposed to do an art project for a charity auction for blind puppies, so I couldn't possible get you a draft of the manuscript until next week.

If you can convince others of your unflinching commitment to a staggering workload, they will have to understand that you really can't take on any more.

Or maybe you've been there, done that. Like Stephen King, who explained why he was thinking of retiring from publishing: "I've killed enough of the world's trees."

This strategy works particularly well at work, I find. If you can convince others of your unflinching commitment to a staggering workload, they will have to understand that you really can't take on any more. You can emulate some of the quirks of the office busy bee. Every workplace has one, that person who shows up two hours before anyone else and talks ad nauseum about this and that project, and things taking longer than expected, etc. Pick up the boasting, but drop the workload. Come in early, sure, for three whole days in a row exactly five minutes earlier than the boss. (If your boss is the busy bee, oh god, I pity thee.) Talk about everything you're up to, with extra padding and some moaning about the difficult (and tedious, and time-consuming) details.

Do other things to make everyone see that you are so busy they won't even think of asking you to do anything else.

Do other things to make everyone see that you are so busy they won't even think of asking you to do anything else. This includes putting your boss on hold for long periods of time while you solve a pressing "problem." Also includes spending a lot of time hovering over the copier and fax machine diligently removing paper jams. And lingering at the file drawers with huge piles of papers from your desk as you look extremely organized. If worse comes to worse, increase your trips to the bathroom. And if you really run out of stuff to do, offer to go out and get coffee for everyone, and take a 20 minute break on the way. While you're gone, they'll probably give that big project to someone else. Anything to avoid more work on your plate.

I would also like to take a brief moment to talk about being a "servant of two masters." If you are unlucky enough to be in the awkward (and with all the personnel cuts going around, increasingly common) position of having more than one boss, you are allowed to feel sorry for yourself for exactly two minutes. After that, my friend, the onus is on you to take matters into your own hands and improve your lot. Moliere said it best, "The greater the obstacle, the more glory in overcoming it."

"The greater the obstacle, the more glory in overcoming it."

Two or more bosses often have some kind of power play going on between them. Does one make more money? Occupy a higher rung on the corporate ladder? Manipulate this to the hilt. When one boss asks you to complete a task, always claim you're in the middle of an urgent job for the other one, and offer with a deep sigh to drop everything for the new project. But let them know you'll have to break the news to the other boss, and hint that you don't know how it'll go over.

Show, Don't Tell

In acting and writing classes, you hear this a lot. Nothing drives a point home so much as action. You can talk and talk about being a fabulous cook or lover, but nothing's going to really drive home the point like the soufflé or the sex itself. In this case, you need a little bit of action that leads to a lot of loafing. These are the times when doing something poorly might just get you out of having to do it at all.

Doing something poorly might just get you out of having to do it at all.

I had a housemate once who was really bad at doing dishes. It's not that she wouldn't wash her dirty dishes, it was *how* she washed them that was bad. She'd use cold water and not enough soap (I think trying to save the environment figured into the strange logic) so all the dishes would have bits of spaghetti sauce or just a weird sheen to them that made me queasy. I had to wash them again before I could eat off of them without dry heaving. Eventually, I just started doing her dishes too, because I figured I was saving myself a second washing.

The wonderful kids' books about a maid named Amelia Bedelia by Peggy Parrish should be your guide in this. She is the literal-minded housekeeper. When she dresses a chicken, she puts it in the baby's clothes. When she weeds the garden, she replants the weeds. And when asked to get the spots out of a shirt, she carefully cuts every polka dot out of it.

So when your mother/wife/husband gives you a list of errands, be creative in messing it all up:

Pick up the dry cleaning. And then put it back down. It's heavy, sheesh!

Shovel the sidewalk. Go and get both shovels, you know, the nice new one and the crappy one that nobody wants to throw away in the vain hope that two people will want to shovel at once. Then go around and knock on neighbors' doors and borrow a few more shovels and lay them all down end to end along the sidewalk. Consider the walkway shoveled.

Empty the dishwasher. First make sure the dishes in the washer are dirty, and then put them away on top of and among the clean ones. Claim you didn't see any dirt on them so how were you supposed to know?

Tidy up the garage. Take the Tidy brand cat litter, and lightly dust it over everything in the garage, including inside the car—that's sure to make an impression.

So much of this showing-not-telling stuff I learned when I started temping right out of college. Temp jobs are a wonderful environment for testing out excuses because if they are so outlandish as to get you fired, it really doesn't matter. There are plenty of other temp jobs and even if your agency gets fed up there are plenty of other agencies.

On your first day of a temp job you have a lot of work to do. And I do not mean the work you are getting paid to do. But if you do this preliminary work right, they will henceforth pay you to surf the internet, print color photos of your brand new nephew, and replenish your home office with post-it notes, file folders, and a rainbow of highlighters.

First, and this is very important, you must not give away your inclination to be a big fat faking manipulating user. You must arrive fifteen minutes early in perfectly appropriate business attire with a good attitude and an (apparent) willingness to work your tushy off. As someone walks you through the job, you want to demonstrate some impressive skills (like knowing a shortcut or two in MS PowerPoint) and give lip service to your willingness to learn and your ability to "pick up most things very quickly."

Don't go too far here. Someone once said brevity is the soul of faking. Or something like that. If it seems like you know more about the job than the person who is actually supposed to do it but happens to be out sick or taking a vacation, that could be bad. For you and for them. Have a heart. Don't show them up. You don't want to give anyone the idea that they should actually give you a full days worth of work to do. As soon as you've established yourself as a well-meaning, semi-talented temp, you're going to want to start dropping the ball. I mean the call. Well, both, if possible. But do it in the nicest way possible, of course, and always be very apologetic. You are relying on the hard and fast rule that no one wants to teach a temp how to do anything. You're only going to be there for a day or two, so it's a waste of everyone's time.

If you have to cover phones, this is great. Drop one call as you transfer. Then, if the person calls back, apologize profusely and ask if they can hold on a minute while you read the instruction book on transferring them to voicemail. Then come back on in twenty seconds or so and as them if they want to keep holding cause you've almost got it or just call back tomorrow when the person you're filling in for will be back in the office. I guarantee they'll want to call back another time.

You may be able to get away with a lot more than you think you can. One friend of mine (who will remain nameless) padded his hours, stole office supplies, printed out and copied hundreds of pages of personal stuff, was reimbursed for expensive meals for months, all as a TEMP, before they asked him to leave. And when they did, they apologized for letting him go and said they really liked him.

It's pretty hard to fire someone these days. This is bad for employers, but good for you. Unless you're an employer. In which case you could just skip the rest of this chapter and go back and reread the one on household excuses.

Not Being Prepared (On Purpose)

When you're sick of everybody calling you for those "pot-luck" dinners and you just want to go and not bother going to the grocery store and doing a lot of cooking beforehand, offer to bring hors d'œuvres. Then show up half an hour late with half the ingredients you need. That'll show them. Or bring a meaty pasta dish for the group of vegans. Or a nutty carrot cake for the family who's allergic to nuts. Then you can take it home and eat it yourself!

Some people lack the gene I like to call the "getting-ready-for-your-day" gene. This provides wonderful excuses for not making it to work or school on time (or at all). It also gives you some leeway for not being prepared, as you basically cannot be relied upon to get everything together at once. This gene is also closely linked in the scientific studies I do in my big fake imaginary head with the "losing-crap-wherever-you-go gene."

You brought a little plastic holder full of number two pencils to take your SAT test, but it must have fallen out of your back when you had to dig around for the bus pass you forgot in your other pants.

My mom still remembers the first "chapter book" she read on her own, or at least she thinks she does—*The Adventures of Tom Sawyer.* I've been hearing about this book since I was about seven, the age my mother claims to have been when she read it. (I have no reason to doubt she was that young—but what was her mother thinking?) Among the many, many things my mother has had to say about this book to me over the years, here's what stuck most—you guessed it—whitewashing the fence. *Tom Sawyer* may be out of fashion as a children's novel, but I will say this for the guy. He's probably the best example ever of the get-someone-else-to-do-it and take-all-the-credit school of excuses. So he's supposed to paint the fence. And I think he even starts to do it.

And then he announces that only he is allowed to white-wash the fence—it's a very special privilege. So, of course, pretty soon all his friends are clamoring to have a go at it. Well, it's so special, that I think he not only gets them to finish the job—and takes the praise from Aunt Polly—but he also charges them for the privilege.

So any time you have an onerous task, you might ask yourself if you can A) make it look appealing to someone else, B) use reverse psychology to get them to do it by saying they can't, and C) maybe even get them to give you money or something else for the privilege. My mom says they should teach this little portion of the novel in business school, that it's some of the best management advice she's ever read. Yeah, like she reads business books!

So any time you have an onerous task, you might ask yourself if you can A) make it look appealing to someone else, B) use reverse psychology to get them to do it, by saying they can't, and C) maybe even get them to give you money or something else for the privilege.

By the way, I'm writing this little bit on Tom Sawyer from my mom's like fifty-year-old memory of the book. So any inaccuracies from the actual story are, you guessed it, not my fault—all hers.

Chapter 8

All's Fair

in

LOVE

Ah, love. That greasy goo that makes the world go 'round. The birds sing louder, colors are brighter, the twitter in your stomach verges on nausea. I haven't mentioned it in this book yet, but it should have occurred to you by now: being in love can be a pretty great excuse all by itself. An excuse for, say, getting a dumb tattoo, for acting like an idiot, for not hanging out with the guys, for spending all your money and getting yourself into a hole of debt that only bankruptcy can partially remedy.

But, as the man Shakespeare says, "The course of true love never did run smooth." In fact, most of the time I find love is fraught with trouble from start to finish. Ergo, you're going to need some good excuses.

The Beginning

I have never understood pick-up lines. Call me a prude, but I cannot imagine those things working. I know a married couple who met when he was bartending and she was a customer. She asked if he liked his job and he replied, "Yeah, I like it, but I'd rather be home shaving your legs." That, to me, is kind of gross. But I guess it worked for her. The point is, clever or not,

Being in love can be a pretty great excuse all by itself.

you may have to have a quick and definitive excuse for not pursuing a conversation, not getting out on the dance floor, and especially for not going on that first date (we'll talk about getting out of second dates in a moment). So never fear, the lame excuse is here.

The lame excuse conveys disdain without being prissy. It's funny. It can let 'em down gentle or slam 'em down hard. And overall, it keeps things light but maintains control of the situation.

Excuses for not giving out your telephone number

By the way, I don't think you should ever give out your number. Seriously. If you like someone you should just get their number. Then you can decide whether you want to call them when the alcohol-induced shimmer has worn off.

So you could always just say, sorry, I don't give out my number. But that's sort of plain Jane, really. Sass it up.

- "I haven't paid my cell phone bill, so you'll just get a funny message that says, 'Sorry, the person you are trying to reach is a deadbeat loser and can't afford to pay for the minutes accrued yapping last month. Please try again when the next paycheck clears.'"

- "I forgot the password so I never check my voicemail. So you'll just get a funny voice saying, 'Sorry, this mailbox is full. There are messages in here from 1997. Messages that have never been heard. Important messages. I am the "voice" in voicemail and I feel dejected. I feel like life has no meaning. Goodbye.'"

- "My boyfriend/brother/father is a Hell's Angel and monitors my voicemail. But I'm sure he'd love to meet you."

- "I'd love to but my dog ate the phone. Seriously. He's a dachshund—they eat anything."

Or you could give them your number. I mean, your "number." Who's the wiser if you're a little tipsy and you accidentally switch around the digits a bit? As long as the area code seems reasonable, old Joe Sleazeball won't have a clue 'til he tries it later on.

If you live in New York, there's actually something called the reject hotline, which is a number you can give out instead of your actual number. When skeezy pickup artists call this bogus number, they reach a recording that says "You've been REJECTED!" It's always nice to have someone else do your dirty work for you. It gives you the feeling of living on an English country estate at the turn of the century. Or of being a higher up in the most powerful crime family in Chicago.

If you live outside of New York, you could either do all the singles in your area a favor and set up a voicemail account and record a rejection message, or you could just look up the number for a suicide hotline in your area. Then you can give that number out, and anyone who calls it will have someone to talk to when they realize you have cruelly rejected them and they are crushed. Or maybe they'll be so offended by your presumption that you broke their heart that they'll just get over the whole thing real fast.

So you got a little tipsy and the lighting was bad and you actually did give out your bona fide number. But you really, really can't face going on an actual date with the dufus who's called three times now. So you need a few reasons you can't go out. The lamer the better.

- **"I'm converting my calendar watch from Julian to Gregorian."**

- **"My grandfather died and I have to travel to Iceland for the funeral."**

- **"I have to rotate my crops. I devised the plan based on medieval tradition."**

- "I'm staying home to work on my cottage cheese sculpture. And I'm afraid the mold is spreading."

- "I'm building a pig from a kit." (I don't know what this means, but maybe that's the charm in it.)

- "I have to take my parakeet to the vet. She's got a terrible cough." (This is totally real. My parakeet that I got for my birthday when I was six died from getting pneumonia and had a hacking cough. It was so traumatizing that I still flinch when a bird comes too close to me.)

- "I'm observing National Apathy Week."

- "My uncle escaped again. He was last seen in Florida with the nozzle and torn-off part of a gas hose trailing behind his car."

The Date

Okay, so maybe you went on the first date. Maybe you're an eternal optimist, or too polite to say no, or just plain desperate. But maybe you had a bad date.

Somebody I know met a guy through an online dating service. They emailed and then talked on the phone, and one of the things he said was that he was a runner and wanted to run a marathon. When they met for coffee, he showed up and he was huge. Really big, and I don't mean tall. She said his shoe was untied and she pointed it out but he couldn't get over his own bulk to tie it, so he asked her to do it for him! When she asked him about being a runner he said, "Oh, yeah, I'm definitely going to do that some day."

There's bad and then there's really bad. If your date starts talking about his affinity for torturing kittens or wearing his mother's panties, you're going to have to think fast. Excuse yourself to the bathroom, where you should stay for a good ten minutes. Tease your hair a bit and rub your eyes until they're puffy and a little watery. Then come back to the table clutching your stomach and say you're so sorry but you've got a terrible case of food poisoning, probably from some bad smoked salmon you had on your bagel this morning. Talk about your diarrhea and your vomit in some detail, and then hightail it out of there, checking the rear view all the way.

And if you made it through the first date, but you just can't face another one? More lame excuses!

- "I'm running off to Yugoslavia with a foreign-exchange student."

- "I'm uncomfortable when I'm alone or with others."

- "I'm being deported."

- "I have conjunctivitis, gonorrhea, herpes, and syphilis. You don't mind, do you?"

The Middle

Excuses within relationships—reasons you stay with someone your mother and best friends hate, training your significant other, getting out of any trouble you've caused, you naughty boy/naughty girl.

Okay, so maybe you actually found someone, you lucky [insert appropriate "b" curse word here]. And maybe you thought you wouldn't need any more excuses. But you were wrong. If there's one thing you should have gleaned by now it's that you pretty much always need excuses. That's right, like you're supposed to eat five servings of fruits and vegetables every day. Well, I'm shooting for five a day too. At least five. If it's a bad day, you're going to need more.

Why do you stay with that fool who treats you like dog dirt? Your mother and best friend hate him/her, you're miserable, and your cat has even started peeing on the bed in silent, stinky protest. I overheard this once in a bar:

"Why are you still with him?"

"Well, um, we have an amazing apartment."

"Oh, pu-leeze. You can't stay with someone forever for their *apartment*."

"Um, what city do you live in? Because I live in New York. Yes, you can stay with someone for their marble countertops, central air, Japanese soaking tub. Yes, I am that shallow." [Special thanks to Daniel Reitz, because this is adapted dialogue from his play *Three Sisters*.]

Is there something your partner does that just drives you insane? A catalyst for those fights where you both sulk around in a funk for three days? Well, remember training your boss to know that you weren't reachable and really can't be relied upon to do any work? Now it's time for your husband or wife or boyfriend or girlfriend. I heard somewhere about a woman who spent a lot of time with trainers of wild and exotic animals. The basic theory is to give ecstatic praise and reinforcement when the animal does something right. And when the wild beast does something wrong, like chew off your pinky finger, you're just supposed to ignore it. A negative reaction of any kind is reinforcement—feeding energy into the problem. So say goodbye to your pinky finger but do not shed a tear.

This can be a sneaky way to deal with other people's excuses. When I'm flaking out, my husband has started to just ignore my excuses and carry on as though I never said anything. Then, when I finally get around to doing whatever it was I said I would, he throws me a protein-rich biscuit and claps enthusiastically. I think it's starting to work, though I'm gaining a little weight.

Excuse Clinic

I'm not naming any names here, but I know some people who have been dating, shacking up, screwing like newlyweds, and fighting like married people for coming up on a decade. What's their excuse for not popping the question? Well, they've got plenty of good ones, and I'm not saying you have to get married, but what happens if one of you wants to get hitched and the other needs to bide some time?

You could mention that hardly any marriages work out these days—in fact, some might say getting married is a good way to screw up a perfectly good relationship. There are plenty of real-life examples to cite here.

But I don't think that's good enough. Maybe try: You can't afford a big enough diamond.

She's a size "queen." What can you say? (I ain't saying she's a gold digger.) *So get off your broke ass and make some money!*

But the best yet, ripped from the headlines, that I've heard from more than one celeb couple about why they can't get it together to tie the knot even though they have three kids and six houses between them . . .

"As long as gay couples cannot get married legally in this country, we're not getting married either." [Brad Pitt]

That's a good one. Get off the hook for a worthy cause, people.

> **Brad Pitt once said: "As long as gay couples cannot get married legally in this country, we're not getting married either."**

Quickies—When You Get So Excited You Have to Drop Everything and Just Do It.

Get your mind out of the gutter! I'm talking about weddings.

Britney Spears got married in Vegas because she wanted to know what it would feel like.

Brit, when I was seven, I licked a telephone pole in negative three degree weather in Minnesota because I wanted to see what it felt like. And even then, I knew it was probably a stupid idea. But pledging undying love and fidelity 'til death or lawyers do us part? Nuh-uh.

Because it seemed like a good idea at the time. In Las Vegas, the chapels stay open all night. You can do a drive through wedding. The busboy from the diner can give you away, in the nude, and then you can have a ceremony performed entirely in the Klingon language. In this land of ultra weirdness, it might not seem so strange, especially after an evening of partying, to marry that childhood friend with buck teeth and dirty toenails. I forgive you. Well, I sort of get it. Actually, no, you're kind of an idiot.

It seemed like a good idea at the time.

I love that Richard Burton and Liz Taylor decided to get married to each other again. I like to think it's because they were staying at The Old Drover's Inn in upstate New York. That place is so romantic I considered marrying the owner when I was there. He's mad cute, but gay and totally taken. All the good ones, my friends, all the good ones. And, to quote my favorite movie star, until gay couples can legally marry in this country, I won't marry a gay man, either! Wait, what?

Fighting

Ever go overboard in a knock-down drag-out fight with your bestest loved one?

Well, maybe you can take comfort from this—I sure hope you haven't gone this far. Ryan Haddon gave her husband at the time, the actor Christian Slater, a cut that required 20 stitches after a brawl in their Vegas hotel room. But they later agreed and publicly announced that she accidentally hit him with a glass while trying to throw water in his face. Huh. I guess that's sort of a good excuse for giving your true love a big fat scar.

And, of course, I can tell you're thinking from all angles here. Fighting with your significant other can mean big-time excuses in other areas of your life, too. I know a couple who occasionally get carried away in their dramatics, and usually it ends when one of them storms out in a huff. Well, one time they *both* stormed out, he out the front and she out the back, both slamming the door hard for emphasis. Both indignant, both sure of being morally superior, both *forgetting their keys*. Needless to say, they formed an even stronger bond as they stayed up until four in the morning trying to break into their house together. They could do nothing the next day because they were exhausted (and also needed to stay home and have some nice make-up nookie). And they had a great story to back it up.

Bad Boys, Bad Girls

You have acted like a total buffoon. You deserve no mercy. But you should at least have the decency to come up with a proper excuse.

> "I wasn't kissing her. I was whispering in her mouth."
> — Chico Marx

What was Hugh Grant's excuse for visiting a trannie prostitute while engaged to Liz Hurley? I think he just flipped his hair to the other side of his forehead and grinned sheepishly. And it worked. Weird.

Excuse Clinic

Caught kissing someone you shouldn't?

Good: "Sure I was kissing her, but it was part of the scene. It's only acting, honey."

Better: "That's my cousin, I haven't seen her in years and I just ran into her. Don't be gross."

Best: from Chico Marx, reportedly said when his wife caught him kissing a chorus girl: "I wasn't kissing her. I was whispering in her mouth."

The bestest: "I kissed her, but it made me realize I don't even like girls anymore. I'm gay and I'm leaving you."

Speaking of calling it quits . . .

The End

Breaking up is hard to do, but easier with these excuses to lend a hand.

Well, there are all the basic platitudes that we've always relied upon.

"We've grown apart."

"It's not you, it's me."

"The spark has faded."

"You don't treat me like you used to do."

and

"I hate you and I can't stand the way you crunch your cornflakes."

"I hate you and I can't stand the way you crunch your cornflakes. I can't look at your big head for another minute without doing something I'm going to regret."

Leaving Someone at the Altar

Or maybe things get a bit out of hand, and you're headed for saying I do's. Maybe you're not ready. Or you thought you were, but really you're not. Or you realized you're still in love with your kindergarten teacher and you need to try to find her and see if she feels the same way about you. You have to retreat without remorse, and everybody's going to have to move on with their lives.

Not least of whom will be whoever's shelled out the cash for this wedding.

- "My car broke down on the way to the service. I got out to look under the hood and oil squirted up onto my tux. I called a tow truck and when we got to the shop, there was a bird in a cage. She looked so cooped up and sad, and the owner of the place said she never sings. I thought it was all a sign."

- "It's not you, it's me. I mean, It's not your fault, it's just that I'm blaming you."

- "I wanted to stop you from making a big mistake. I have hereditary late-onset insanity on both sides of my family, and I couldn't bear the thought of going crazy and you having to take care of me for the rest of our lives."

- "I met someone wonderful at the strip club we went to for my bachelorette party. Someone who works there."

The great thing about getting married is that it's a way for two people who are in love to open up their relationship to the care and guidance of their community of friends and family. The bad thing about opening up your intimate coupling in this way is that you each have a mother. And that adds up to two mothers-in-law. More, if you count any step-mothers-in-law who might be hanging around. And mothers-in-law can be opinionated, nasty, annoying, or just plain crazy. When you're headed to the altar, you may as well just accept that you're marrying this whole family-warts, mothers, grandmothers and all.

So if that's just the last straw, you might have to explain:

- "Your mother hates me. She's always going to hate me and she'll eventually turn you against me. We don't have a chance in hell."

- "All women become their mothers when they get older. I hate your mother. If you turn into her I'm going to be married to your mother, and I would rather be roasted over a spit while evil children shove peppercorns under my skin."

- "You know how all women turn into their mothers when they get older? And you know how you hate my mother? Well, I'm just going to turn into an exact replica of her, so we might as well end this now and save you the trouble of hating me later on."

Speaking of mothers. Maybe she could come in handy. Maybe she could break the news for you, so you don't have to. It's awkward showing up at your own wedding and then leaving right away. Just pull a no-show altogether, and let her explain.

Chapter 9

THE

Little Chapter

of

BIG BUTS

Or, Excuses We Tell Ourselves

I was recently over at a friend's house visiting with her and her two-year-old daughter, and at one point the little girl had an accident in her pants. When her mom asked her why this happened she explained, "I'm sorry Mama, I'm too busy to use the potty today."

I know the feeling.

So much to do, so little time. Maybe if I had diapers I could get more done in my day, too.

We all have excuses we tell ourselves (and then also share with others) about why we couldn't—or didn't— do better today. We all have goals and dreams and visions of ourselves, maybe twenty pounds lighter, maybe running triumphantly across the finish line of a marathon. But I'm here to encourage you to be realistic. Sure, have some goals. But don't make them grandiose. Give yourself some room to grow—small steps, if you will, on the road to fulfillment of a better you. And in the meantime, it's probably just fine to eat some candy, slack off on your pushups, and hey, maybe even throw yourself a party for your half birthday. Or your cat's half birthday. Whatevs.

However, if you are making excuses for your love of hard drugs or your inability to feed your children, or you are a certain tennis

"I'm sorry Mama, I'm too busy to use the potty today."

player who was quite famous in the 80s and couldn't take personal responsibility for losing a single match ever, then you should maybe take a long hard look in the mirror. And get some simpler vices.

Dieting — or Why I Like to Eat All the Things I Shouldn't and Don't Eat All the Things I Should.

I like chocolate. The darker the better. And everything tastes better with butter. Period. I've tried every diet and they all suck. You feel terrible about yourself, and also you just feel terrible because the whole theory of dieting is you have to burn more calories than you take in. That's what I like to call a deficit, people, and if it's not good for my bank account, and it's not good for the country, how can it be good for my body? When I take

137

in more than I put out, I like to think I'm building up my own little investment portfolio, right around my middle.

There are so many reasons for not starting my latest diet. I could fill a whole book. Some studies show that diet drinks with artificial sweeteners like aspartame stimulate the appetite. Thus: "I can't start my diet today, I accidentally drank three diet Mr. Pibbs and now I'm freaking starving."

If I lose a bunch of weight I won't have anything to wear, and I can't afford a new wardrobe.

Besides, if I lose a bunch of weight I won't have anything to wear, and I can't afford a new wardrobe.

In fact, I've been measured for my costume and they tell me it can't be altered. If you don't have any excuse to wear a costume, you may say you've been measured for your uniform. But "costume" is really so much more evocative, how can you pass it up? No need to offer any further details. It could be for a costume ball, for Halloween, for your local production of *The King and I*. What do they know?

If they ask you why it can't be altered, say it's made out of taffeta. I had a bridesmaid's dress once that was made out of taffeta, and the seamstress (my aunt Pearl) took it in too much. Really, it was all her fault. The lumberjack days pancake breakfast had nothing to do with it, how dare you insinuate such a thing?! Anyway, long story short, it had to be let out. And here's the thing about taffeta. It shows all the needle holes from the previous seam. So there was a nice little line down both my sides that screamed "I was too fat for my dress so they had to make it bigger!" Let me tell you, I kept my arms firmly at my sides for that whole ceremony. And the other thing about taffeta is that as soon as you start to sweat (and with your arms pressed to your sides this is inevitable) your sweat shows up as a huge dark lake of destruction seeping from under your pits. I couldn't even do the chicken dance I was so mortified. Who invented taffeta? And why do people make bridesmaids' dresses out of it? My god, the stuff should be outlawed. There are plenty of perfectly wonderful polyester blends out there these days.

And as for healthy foods? Broccoli makes me gassy, don't get me started on tofu, and all the apples at the grocery store are too mealy. I like them crisp. And someone told me once that in their home country (I can't remember where, somewhere in South America?) they have a tradition that you put a bowl of apples on the table, and they soak up all the bad energy in the room. And that's what makes them wither and rot. And if you eat those apples that have been sitting in that bowl, you are consuming every angry word that was spoken, every miserable thought from that room. You are taking it all into your body. Yuck. So I don't eat apples anymore, or really any fruit at all.

Broccoli makes me gassy, don't get me started on tofu, and all the apples at the grocery store are too mealy. I like them crisp.

Meanwhile, I still have to try to get my recommended daily allowance of fruits and vegetables, but all I can face are jelly donuts and French fries. There's fruit in jelly, right? And fried potato is a vegetable, right? And if I put ketchup on them, that counts for two, no?

Okay, we can get all scientific about it if we must. Mari Sandell and Paul Breslin of Monell Chemical Senses Center in Philadelphia, Pennsylvania, wanted to test a theory they came up with about people like me who don't like certain healthful foods that others find delicious. They gave willing victims seventeen raw vegetables known to be rich in glucosinolates—stuff like broccoli, cauliflower, Brussels sprouts, radishes, and turnips. Some people have really strong reactions to the bitterness in these foods—they really taste *more* icky to some of us than others. So there. I can't eat vegetables. My taste receptor genes code for a form of TAS2R that's sensitive to glucosinolates.

We can't eat healthy foods because they taste more icky to us than they are to others.

So if I can't feel so hot about dieting or eating the right foods, then maybe it's time to feel better about my bod just the way it is. You know how there are all those ads for anti-cellulite creams and treatments and gels? They make you feel like cellulite is a terrible disease that normal women don't get, but because you're cursed with it you have to spend half your disposable income on eradicating it. Well I am here to tell you that three out of four women have cellulite, and that to me makes it officially normal. Those 25% who are blob free are either lying to the statisticians, or they already laid down the cash for the nip and tuck.

Smoking, Drinking, Alcohol, Sex, Drugs, and Rock 'n' Roll

Wait, is all that bad for you, even the last few? Tarnation, how's a girl to have any fun at all?

When you wake up the next morning so hung over you can't actually maintain a vertical position for more than fifteen seconds, you ask yourself why did I get smashed at that wedding/bar mitzvah/office Christmas party? There was free alcohol. And I'm really poor. I don't socialize well. Someone must have spiked my drink. If this is sounding too familiar, it might be time to look up your local AA chapter. They're everywhere.

Whitney Houston did us all the favor of sharing her reason for not using crack, even though she admitted to using a laundry list of other controlled substances. She said, "Crack is cheap. I make too much money to use crack. Crack is wack."

And as for smoking, I never started, but my friends tell me you can use a lot of the same excuses for not dieting. You'll start tomorrow, you're too busy and quitting would just take your time and energy. You have an oral fixation for which smoking is the least worrisome outlet. And the poverty excuse can come in handy here, too. I can't stop smoking because I can't afford to throw away another ashtray.

Personal Accomplishments and Success (Hey, ease up on these. They'll bite you in the butt, I swear.)

These are the excuses we make to ourselves for not fulfilling our potential at work, at school, in sports, or in our creative endeavors. And I say, *watch out*. Make excuses for stupid stuff, like not doing the dishes, or getting married spur of the moment in Vegas, but this stuff is important. If you're making too many excuses for failing to live up to your own intelligence and talent, knock it off, already!

If you're making too many excuses for failing to live up to your own intelligence and talent, knock it off, already!

Did you know that tall people earn more money? Nobody knows exactly why, but people theorize maybe they have better self-esteem or confidence than short people, or maybe it's that others view them as leaders.

Who knows. All I know is, if you're short, you've got a great excuse for not getting that raise. (It couldn't possibly be because you've been reading this book and weaseling out of actually working for a living. Heck no.) The good news is, short people live longer than tall people. But I guess that means you should budget. Because even though you haven't made as much money, you're going to have to make it stretch for a longer retirement.

> **"It's a great excuse and luxury, having a job and blaming it for your inability to do your own art."**

When the golfer Michelle Wie came in dead last at the European Masters tournament a while back, she had a good excuse. She was paying attention to her studies. A fine excuse, if you ask me. "My school like totally piled on the homework last week, and I had to bring much of it with me to Switzerland, so I wasn't able to practice like I usually do because I was working on this geography report."

John McEnroe is famous for making excuses, and not good ones like that. For every match he lost, there was something outside of his control that made all the difference. A bad call, the weather, noise in the stands, an injury. Unfortunately, this excuse-making seems to have carried over into all aspects of his life, which probably makes him not so much fun to be around.

The painter Julian Schnabel said, "It's a great excuse and luxury, having a job and blaming it for your inability to do your own art. When you don't have to work, you are left with the horror of facing your own lack of imagination and your own emptiness. A devastating possibility when finally time is your own."

Which brings me to a good point. I hope this book will inspire you to make creative excuses. Not excuses to hide out because you're afraid to live your life, but excuses to get yourself out of the crappy parts of your life so you can get on with living the fabulous and important parts.

Which brings me to…

Excuses to Have Fun for No Reason

You need to have fun in your life. And with so few sanctioned holidays out there, sometimes you have to make up your own little reason to call in a sick day or have some friends over for dinner or go on vacation. These holidays and special events are underknown and under-appreciated, and it's time for that to change.

When I was a kid, my godmother kidnapped me from school one day. Of course, it was all prearranged with my parents and the school knew about it, but I had no clue and it felt very clandestine and fancy. She presented me with a handmade "get out of school free card" and whisked me away for no particular reason. We had lunch, went for a walk, picked flowers. I was on cloud nine.

So if you have kids, you can pretty much make up a silly excuse any time to throw a party.

So if you have kids, you can pretty much make up a silly excuse any time to throw a party. Half birthdays, pets' birthdays. The 3rd of March is Girl's Day and the 5th of May is Children's Day in Japan. Also feel free to celebrate the birthdays of fictional characters. July 31st is Harry Potter's birthday, and I know he'd be hurt if we didn't have a cake. I have a friend with a toddler who had a "goodbye to bottles and pacifiers" party. They had a nice cake, and then the little girl put all her bottles and pacifiers into a box to send them to children who needed them. She was thirteen at the time. Just kidding.

Anyway, the idea is, use some of the excuses in this book to finagle yourself some time to, I don't know, go on vacation, play the lottery, go dancing, blow off work on the first day of spring, stay in bed all day except for a dip in the bubble bath.

And here, friends, is where we come to a close.

Take care of yourself, don't take yourself too seriously, and become an A-list excuse monger. Remember: you deserve it, and it's about time.

When I was little we used to go on torturous car trip summer vacations with the stinky dog and fifteen-year-old shocks in the station wagon, and the only beacon of frilly levity was the never-ending book of Mad Libs™ (if you could hold down your fast food long enough to finish one while reading in the back seat). Mad Libs are those crazy stories with a bunch of words left blank. One person acts as scribe, and only she knows what the story is about. She goes around the room, or the car, and asks for words that satisfy the part of speech—noun, verb, adjective, etc., and of course the results are hilarious.

So, I leave you with this, and by now you should be at the top of your excuse game, so try it with your friends, and feel free to make up your own (and thereby get nothing done at work or school).

Excuses Fib Lib

I'm so sorry to be _____ today.

crappy state of being

You see, I only got _____ hours of sleep

fraction or decimal

after getting off work as a _____ .

job that stinks

I really had to _____ ,

gross bodily function

and the _____ that was coming out

viscous liquid

was not to be believed. Furthermore, as I drove past

_____'s house,

famous person

I was pulled over by a _____ cop.

pejorative adjective

Things got pretty _____
                              lurid adjective

as I described my _____'s
                              family member

_____.
        unpleasant surgical procedure

Needless to say, the cop hauled my ass off to

_____.
        place you don't want to go

So not only am I late, I'm _____
                                    crappy state of being

and really _____.
                horrifying state of being

Thanks so much for understanding.

May I be excused now?

About the Author

ADDIE JOHNSON grew up in San Francisco, went east to Vassar College, and never bothered to leave New York. She's an actor and helps run Rising Phoenix Rep, a small developmental theatre company. She's also an editor and writer, and this is her first book. She lives in Brooklyn with her family, who never believe her excuses. That doesn't stop her from trying.

To Our Readers

CONARI PRESS, an imprint of Red Wheel/Weiser, publishes books on topics ranging from spirituality, personal growth, and relationships to women's issues, parenting, and social issues. Our mission is to publish quality books that will make a difference in people's lives—how we feel about ourselves and how we relate to one another. We value integrity, compassion, and receptivity, both in the books we publish and in the way we do business.

Our readers are our most important resource, and we value your input, suggestions, and ideas about what you would like to see published. Please feel free to contact us, to request our latest book catalog, or to be added to our mailing list.

Conari Press

An imprint of Red Wheel/Weiser, LLC

500 Third Street, Suite 230

San Francisco, CA 94107

www.redwheelweiser.com